Designing and Implementing a Server Infrastructure Exam 70-413

Lab Manual

WITHDRAWN

Patrick Regan

WILEY

EXECUTIVE EDITOR	John Kane
EDITORIAL ASSISTANT	Jessy Moor
TECHNICAL REVIEWERS	Brian Svidergol
	Ron Handlon
SENIOR PRODUCTION & MANUFACTURING MANAGER	Janis Soo
ASSOCIATE PRODUCTION MANAGER	Joyce Poh

www.wiley.com/college/microsoft or
call the MOAC Toll-Free Number: 888-764-7001 (U.S. & Canada only)

ISBN 978-1-118-78915-5

Printed in the United States of America

BRIEF CONTENTS

CONTENTS

LAB 1
DESIGNING AN AUTOMATED SERVER INSTALLATION STRATEGY

THIS LAB CONTAINS THE FOLLOWING EXERCISES AND ACTIVITIES:

Exercise 1.1   Planning and Selecting Images (Data Collection and Tracking Project)

Exercise 1.2   Installing Windows Assessment and Deployment Kit (ADK)

Exercise 1.3   Installing and Configuring Windows Deployment Services (WDS)

Exercise 1.4   Using SysPrep

Lab Challenge   Designing and Planning an Automated Server Installation Strategy
(Home Security Product Project)

BEFORE YOU BEGIN

The lab environment consists of student workstations connected to a local area network, along with a server that functions as the domain controller for a domain called contoso.com. The computers required for this lab are listed in Table 1-1.

Table 1-1
Computers required for Lab 1

Computer	Operating System	Computer Name
Server	Windows Server 2012 R2	CRWDC01
Server	Windows Server 2012 R2	CSERVER02

In addition to the computers, you will also need the software listed in Table 1-2 to complete Lab 1.

Table 1-2
Software required for Lab 1

Software	Location
Windows Server 2012 R2 installation disks	\\rwdc01\software
Windows Assessment and Deployment Kit for Windows 8.1	\\rwdc01\software
Lab 1 student worksheet	Lab01_worksheet.docx (provided by instructor)

Working with Lab Worksheets

Each lab in this manual requires that you answer questions, shoot screen shots, and perform other activities that you will document in a worksheet named for the lab, such as Lab01_worksheet.docx. You will find these worksheets on the book companion site. It is recommended that you use a USB flash drive to store your worksheets, so you can submit them to your instructor for review. As you perform the exercises in each lab, open the appropriate worksheet file, fill in the required information, and then save the file to your flash drive.

SCENARIO

After completing this lab, you will be able to:

■ Plan and select images

■ Install Windows Assessment and Deployment Kit (ADK)

■ Install and configure Windows Deployment Services (WDS)

■   Use SysPrep

■   Given a scenario, plan a server deployment

Estimated lab time: 200 minutes

Exercise 1.1	Planning and Selecting Images (Data Collection and Tracking Project)
Overview	In this written exercise, you will read the background information for the Contoso Corporation provided in Appendix A, read the information introduced in this lesson, and then answer the questions below.
Mindset	An image is a single file or other storage device that contains the complete contents and structure of a disk or other data storage device used with computers and other devices. An image is often created from a reference or master computer. However, when you want to deploy Windows to multiple computers, you need to select the type of images, determine the number of images, and determine how you will create and use the images.
Completion time	30 minutes

To accommodate a new line of products, you must deploy 400 new servers in the data center. The servers will be used to keep track of product settings and will constantly collect and analyze data from the sold security products. In addition, if sales increase as planned, you will need to deploy a hundred servers each month over the next year or two.

Of these servers, there are four types:

●   File server – Stores documents and logs

●   Web server – Allows device and user access over the Internet

●   Database server – Allows storage and retrieval of data

●   Application server – Includes applications that allow the management of the system and includes components that process the data.

Answer the following questions.

Question 1	Which type of image—sector-based images or file-based images—should be selected and why?

Question 2	Which type of image (thick, thin, or hybrid) should be used to deploy the servers and why?

| Question 3 | What is the minimum number of images necessary to deploying these servers and why? |

| Question 4 | Which server deployment strategy should be used to deploy these servers (High Touch with Retail Media, High Touch with Standard Image, Lite-Touch, High-Volume Deployment, or Zero-Touch, High-Volume Deployment) and why? |

| Question 5 | Based on your answer to Question 4, which servers are necessary for the deployment and which software components must be run by those servers? |

| Question 6 | When you deploy the four types of servers, how do you specify which roles, features, files, and applications are deployed to the deployed server? |

Exercise 1.2	Installing Windows Assessment and Deployment Kit (ADK)
Overview	In this exercise, you will install Windows Assessment and Deployment Kit (ADK) so that it will be used for future exercises. You will not be guided through each step. Instead, you must determine the best way to deploy the application based on the guidelines provided below.
Mindset	Windows ADK is a collection of tools and documentation designed to help IT professionals deploy Windows operating systems. Windows ADK is ideal for highly customized environments, because the tools in Windows ADK can be used to configure many deployment options.
Completion time	20 minutes

Install Windows ADK to CServer02 with the following components:

- Volume Activation Management Tool (VAMT)

- Windows Performance Toolkit

- Windows Assessment Services

- Microsoft SQL Server 2012 Express

The installation files for the Windows ADK are located in the \\crwdc01\software\Windows Kits folder.

At the end of the installation, on the *Welcome to the Windows Assessment and Deployment Kit for Windows 8.1* page, take a screen shot by pressing Alt+Prt Scr and then paste it into your Lab 1 worksheet file in the page provided by pressing Ctrl+V.

Exercise 1.3	Installing and Configuring Windows Deployment Services (WDS)
Overview	In this exercise, you will install and configure Windows Deployment Services (WDS) so that you can quickly install Windows servers in the future. You will not be guided through each step. Instead, you must determine the best way to deploy the application based on the guidelines provided.
Mindset	WDS is a Windows server role used to deploy windows over the network without little or no user intervention. If the client can perform a PXE boot, you perform an installation over a network with no operating system or local boot device on it. The WDS server will store and help administrators manage the boot image files and operating system image files used in the network installations.
Completion time	60 minutes

Install Windows Deployment Services to CServer02. To store your images and unattended.xml files, create the C:\Software folder on CServer02. The Windows Server 2012 installation disk can be foiund in \\CRWDC01\Software.

When the Windows Deployment Services Configuration has been executed, take a screen shot of the Windows Deployment Services Configuration Wizard by pressing Alt+Prt Scr and then paste it into your Lab 1 worksheet file in the page provided by pressing Ctrl+V.

When you add the Windows Server 2012 R2 Standard image is added to WDS, take a screenshot of the Install Images named node (such as ImageGroup1) showing the install images that have been added by pressing Alt+Prt Scr and then paste it into your Lab 1 worksheet file in the page provided by pressing Ctrl+V.

Lab Challenge	Designing and Planning an Automated Server Installation Strategy (Home Security Product Project)
Overview	You are a new administrator for the Contoso Corporation, which is a leading producer of smart devices for the home, and you need to develop an automated installation strategy. You will read the background information for the Contoso Corporation provided in Appendix A, then read the information presented below, and then describe your solution.
Mindset	As part of a new product line consisting of home security monitoring and medical monitoring equipment for the Contoso Corporation, you need to create hundreds of servers, which will be sold as part of the product and service. Therefore, within the next three months, you will need to deploy several hundred servers for the initial launch and you will need to deploy additional servers as the product becomes more popular.
Completion time	90 minutes

The Contoso Corporation design team is close to finishing up a new product for home security monitoring and medical monitoring equipment. As a new administrator, you are called into your manager's office to discuss this exciting new project. He explains that the product is centered around a server that collects and analyzes information from wireless nodes around the house or worn by an individual. To keep track of data, the server will use Windows Internal Database (WID). As part of the rollout, hundreds of servers will need to be prepared for the product rollout and additional servers will be needed to replace sold inventory.

Your manager wants you to design a solution that can create hundreds of new servers each month. You must work with the design team to create an automated server installation plan that will support this project. The servers will have to be tested by the quality control team before being shipped to customers.

Create a proposal that includes the following sections:

- Purpose of the Project
- Requirements of the Project
- The Proposed Solution

When writing the proposal, you must explain the reasoning behind your choices.

NOTE: This lab challenge will continue into Lab 2.

End of lab.

LAB 2
IMPLEMENTING A SERVER DEPLOYMENT INFRASTRUCTURE

THIS LAB CONTAINS THE FOLLOWING EXERCISES AND ACTIVITIES:

Exercise 2.1   Installing SQL Server 2012 with SP1

Exercise 2.2   Installing and Configuring Microsoft Deployment Toolkit

Exercise 2.3   Installing Configuration Manager

Exercise 2.4   Running the Configure ConfigMgr Integration Wizard

Exercise 2.5   Configuring Configuration Manager

Lab Challenge   Designing and Planning an Automated Server Installation Strategy (Home Security Product Project)

BEFORE YOU BEGIN

The lab environment consists of student workstations connected to a local area network, along with a server that functions as the domain controller for a domain called contoso.com. The computers required for this lab are listed in Table 2-1.

Table 2-1
Computers required for Lab 2

Computer	Operating System	Computer Name
Server	Windows Server 2012 R2	CRWDC01
Server	Windows Server 2012 R2	CSERVER01
Server	Windows Server 2012 R2	CSERVER02

In addition to the computers, you will also need the software listed in Table 2-2 to complete Lab 2.

Table 2-2
Software required for Lab 2

Software	Location
SQL Server 2012 R2	\\crwdc01\software
System Center 2012 R2 Configuration Manager	\\crwdc01\software
Microsoft Deployment Toolkit 2013	\\crwdc01\software
ConfigMgr Download files	\\crwdc01\software
Lab 2 student worksheet	Lab02_worksheet.docx (provided by instructor)

Working with Lab Worksheets

Each lab in this manual requires that you answer questions, shoot screen shots, and perform other activities that you will document in a worksheet named for the lab, such as Lab02_worksheet.docx. You will find these worksheets on the book companion site. It is recommended that you use a USB flash drive to store your worksheets, so you can submit them to your instructor for review. As you perform the exercises in each lab, open the appropriate worksheet file, fill in the required information, and then save the file to your flash drive.

SCENARIO

After completing this lab, you will be able to:

- Install SQL Server 2012 with SP1

- Install and configure Microsoft Deployment Toolkit

- Install Configuration Manager

- Run the Configure ConfigMgr Integration Manager

■ Prepare Configuration Manager to Deploy Windows Server 2012 R2

■ Design and plan an automated server installation strategy

Estimated lab time: 240 minutes

Exercise 2.1	Installing SQL Server 2012 with SP1
Overview	In this exercise, you will install SQL Server 2012 with SP1.
Mindset	SQL Server 2012 with SP1 is required to run Configuration Manager and Virtual Machine Manager (VMM).
Completion time	45 minutes

1. On **CServer01**, log on using the **contoso\administrator** account and the **Pa$$w0rd** password.

2. Right-click **Windows 2012 R2 installation Disk** ISO and choose **Mount**.

3. Using *Server Manager*, click **Manage > Add Roles and Features.**

4. In the **Add Roles and Features** Wizard, click **Next**.

5. On the *Select installation type* page, click **Next**.

6. On the *Select destination server* page, click **Next**.

7. On the *Select server roles* page, click **Next**.

8. On the *Select features* page, select **.NET Framework 3.5 Features** and then click **Next**.

9. On the *Confirm installation selections* page, click **Specify an alternate source path**.

10. In the *Specify Alternate Source path* dialog box, in the *Path* text box, type **E:\Sources\SxS** and then click **OK**.

11. Back on the *Confirm installation selections* page, click **Install**.

12. When the installation is complete, click **Close**.

13. Open **File Explorer** by clicking **File Explorer** on the taskbar.

14. Using File Explorer, navigate to **\\crwdc01\software**.

15. Double-click the SQL Server 2012 with SP1ISO file.

16. On the *SQL Server Installation Center* page, click **Installation** and then click **New SQL Server stand-alone installation or add features to an existing installation**.

17. On the *Setup Support Rules* page, click **OK**.

18. On the *Product Key* page, select **Specify a free edition** and then click **Next**.

19. On the *License Terms* page, select **I accept the license terms** and then click **Next**.

20. On the *Products Updates* page, click **Next**.

21. On the *Setup Support Rules* page, click **Next**.

22. On the *Setup Role* page, click **Next**.

23. On the *Features Selection* page, select **Database Engine Services** and **Management Tools - Complete**. Click **Next**.

24. On the *Installation Rules* page, click **Next**.

25. On the *Instance Configuration* page, answer the following question and then click **Next**.

Question 1	*Which instance is selected and what is it named?*

26. On the *Disk Space Requirements* page, click **Next**.

27. On the *Server Configuration* page, change the account for SQL Server Database Engine from NT Service\MSSQLSERVER to **contoso\administrator**. In the corresponding text box, type **Pa$$W0rd**. Click **Next**.

28. On the *Database Engine Configuration* page, Windows authentication mode is already selected. Click **Add Current User** and then click **Next**.

29. On the *Error Reporting* page, click **Next**.

30. On the *Installation Configuration Rules* page, click **Next**.

31. On the *Ready to Install* page, click **Install**.

32. When the installation is complete, take a screenshot by pressing **Alt+Prt Scr** and then paste it into your Lab 2 worksheet file provided by pressing **Ctrl+V**.

33. Click **Close**.

34. Close the **SQL Server Installation Center** window.

Exercise 2.2	Installing and Configuring Microsoft Deployment Toolkit
Overview	In this exercise, you will install and configure Microsoft Deployment Toolkit. You will then create a deployment share.
Mindset	Microsoft Deployment Toolkit (MDT) 2013 provides end-to-end guidance for planning, building, and deploying of the Windows 8.1 and Windows Server 2012 R2 operating systems. It allows you to deploy Windows using a lite-touch installation or zero-touch installation. MDT allows you to create a deployment share, which contains additional scripts and task sequences to customize the installation process of Windows.
Completion time	20 minutes

1. On **CServer02**, log on using the **contoso\administrator** account and the **Pa$$w0rd** password.

2. Using File Explorer, navigate to **\\crwdc01\software**.

3. Double-click the **MicrosoftDeploymentToolkit2013x64** application. If you are prompted to confirm that you want to run this file, click **Run**.

4. In the Microsoft Deployment Toolkit 2013 Setup wizard, on the *Welcome* page, click **Next**.

5. On the *End-User License Agreement* page, select **I accept the terms in the License Agreement** and then click **Next**.

6. On the *Custom Setup* page, click **Next**.

7. On the *Customer Experience Improvement Program* page, click **Next**.

8. On the *Ready to install Microsoft Deployment Toolkit 2013* page, click **Install**.

9. When the installation is complete, take a screenshot by pressing **Alt+Prt Scr** and then paste it into your Lab 2 worksheet file provided by pressing **Ctrl+V**.

10. Click **Finish**.

11. Click the **Start** button, click the **All Programs** button, and then click **Deployment Workbench**.

12. When the *Deployment Workbench* opens, under *Information Center*, click **Components**.

Question 2	*Which component is required?*

13. Right-click the **Deployment Shares** node and choose **New Deployment Share**.

14. In the *New Deployment Share Wizard*, on the *Path* page, answer the following question and then click **Next**.

Question 3	What is the default deployment share path?

15. On the *Share* folder, click **Next**.

16. On the *Descriptive Name* page, click **Next**.

17. On the *Options* page, click **Next**.

18. On the *Summary* page, click **Next**.

19. When the installation is complete, take a screenshot by pressing **Alt+Prt Scr** and then paste it into your Lab 2 worksheet file provided by pressing **Ctrl+V**.

20. Click **Finish**.

Close Deployment Workbench.

Exercise 2.3	Installing Configuration Manager
Overview	In this exercise, you will install the necessary prerequisites and then you will install Configuration Manager.
Mindset	Configuration Manager allows you to manage your PCs and servers, to keep software up-to-date, to deploy software, to configure settings, and to apply security policies.
Completion time	60 minutes

1. On CServer01, using *Server Manager*, click **Tools > Computer Management**.

2. In *Server Management*, expand the **Local Users and Groups** and then click **Groups**.

3. Double-click **Administrators**.

4. In the *Administrators Properties* dialog box, click **Add**.

5. In the *Select Users, Computers, Services Accounts, or Groups* dialog box, click the **Object Types** button.

6. In the *Object Types* dialog box, select **Computers** and then click **OK**.

7. In the *Enter the object names to select* text box, type **CServer02**.

8. Click **OK** to close the *Administrators Properties* dialog box.

9. On *CServer02*, open **Server Manager**.

10. Click **Manage > Add Roles and Features**.

11. In the *Add Roles and Features Wizard*, on the *Before you begin* page, click **Next**.

12. On the *Select Installation* type page, click **Next**.

13. On the *Select destination server* page, click **Next**.

14. On the *Select server roles* page, click **Next**.

15. On the next few screens, ensure the following is installed:

    - **Internet Information Services (IIS) Manager (Role) with WebDAV, ASP.Net 3.5, ASP.NET 4.5, IIS 6 Management Compatibility (including IIS 6 Metabase Compatibility, and IIS 6 WMI Compatibility)**

    - **.NET Framework 3.5**

    - **.NET Framework 4.0**

    - **Remote Differential Compression**

    - **Background Intelligent Transfer Service (BITS) features**

    Click **Next**.

16. On the *Confirm installation selections* page, if you have to install .NET Framework 3.5, make sure to select the Specify an alternate source path and specify the E:\Sources\SxS path. Then click **Install**.

17. When the feature is installed, click **Close**.

18. Using File Explorer, navigate to **\\crwdc01\software**.

19. Double-click the **System Center 2012 R2 Configuration Manager ISO**.

20. When the ISO file is mounted, open the **\SMSSETUP\BIN\I386** folder and double-click the **extadsch.exe** application.

21. Go back to the root folder of the SCCM mounted drive and double-click the **Splash** HTML application.

22. When the *Microsoft System Center 2012 R2 Configuration Manager* splash screen opens, click **Install**.

23. On the *Before You Begin* page, click **Next**.

24. On the *Available Setup Options* page, click **Install a Configuration Manager primary site** and then click **Next**.

25. On the *Product key* page, select **Install the evaluation edition of this product**. Click **Next**.

26. On the *Microsoft Software License Terms* page, click **I accept these license terms** and then click **Next**.

27. On the *Prerequisite license* page, click **I accept these License Terms for Microsoft SQL Server 2012 Express, Microsoft SQL Server 2012 Native Client, and Microsoft Silverlight** and then click **Next**.

28. On the *Prerequisite Downloads* page, in the top *Path* text box, type **\\rwdc01\software\ConfMgrDownload** and then click **Next**.

29. On the *Server Language Selections* page, click **Next**.

30. On the *Client Language Selection* page, click **Next**.

31. On the *Site and Installation Settings* page, answer the following question and then type the following:

    Site code: **001**

    Site name: **Corporate**

Question 4	What is the path to the installation folder?

32. Click **Next**.

33. On the *Primary Site Installation* page, select **Install the primary site as a stand-alone site** and then click **Next**.

34. When you are prompted confirm that you want to continue, click **Yes**.

35. On the *Database Information* page, in the *SQL Server name (FQDN):* text box, type **CServer01.contoso.com**.

Question 5	What is the database name?

36. Click **Next**.

37. On the *Database information* page, click **Next**.

38. On the *SMS Provider Settings* page, click **Next**.

39. On the *Client Computer Communication Settings* page, select **Configure the communication method on each site system role** and then click **Next**.

40. On the *Site System Roles* page, *Install a management point* and *install a distribution point* is selected. Click **Next**.

41. On the *Customer Experience Improvement Program* page, select **I don't want to join the program at this time** and then click **Next**.

42. On the *Settings Summary* page, click **Next**.

43. If any prerequisite is missing, the SCCM informs you before it starts the installation. Fix all prerequisites. When done, click **Begin install**.

44. When the installation is complete, take a screenshot by pressing **Alt+Prt Scr** and then paste it into your Lab 2 worksheet file provided by pressing **Ctrl+V**.

45. When the installation is complete, click **Close**.

46. Close the **Microsoft System Center 2012 R2 Configuration Manager** splash screen.

47. Click the **Start** button and then click **All Programs > Configuration Manager**.

Close the System Center 2012 R2 Configuration Manager.

Exercise 2.4	Running the Configure ConfigMgr Integration Wizard
Overview	In this exercise, you will run the Configure ConfigMgr Integration Wizard, which will add Microsoft Deployment Toolkit to Configuration Manager.
Mindset	To perform a Zero Touch Deployment, you need to install and configure System Center Configuration Manager.
Completion time	5 minutes

1. Open the **Start Menu**, click **All Programs**, and in the *Microsoft Deployment Toolkit* section, click **Configure ConfigMgr Integration**.

2. In the *Configure ConfigMgr Integration Wizard*, click **Next**.

3. If necessary, modify any options and then click **Next**.

4. On the *Confirmation* page, click **Finish**.

5. Click the Start button and click **All Programs** > **Configuration Manager**.

6. Click the **Software Library** workspace.

7. Expand the **Operating Systems** node and then click **Boot Images**.

8. Take a screenshot by pressing **Alt+Prt Scr** and then paste it into your Lab 2 worksheet file provided by pressing **Ctrl+V**.

Leave System Center 2012 R2 Configuration Manager open for the next exercise.

Exercise 2.5	Configuring Configuration Manager
Overview	In this exercise, you will configure Configuration Manager so that it is ready to deploy a Windows Server 2012 R2, including enabling PXE Support, enabling multicast, creating a task sequence, creating a device collection, and creating an advertisement for the Windows deployment.
Mindset	Before you can deploy an operating system, you need to configure a task sequence, a collection, and an advertisement. The task sequence specifies that an operating system is being deployed and the collection specifies who will receive an operating system. The advertisement brings it all together by specifying when the operating system will be deployed.
Completion time	60 minutes

1. In the *Configuration Manager* console, in the navigation pane (bottom left pane), click **Administration**.

2. In the *Administration* workspace, expand **Overview** and then click **Distribution Points**.

3. Right-click the **CSERVER02.CONTOSO.COM** distribution point and choose **Properties**.

4. In the *Properties* dialog box, click the **PXE** tab.

5. Click to select **Enable PXE support for clients**. When are you are prompted to confirm that you want to enable PXE support for clients, click **Yes**.

6. Click the **Multicast** tab.

7. Select the **Enable multicast to simultaneously send data to multiple clients**.

8. Click **OK** to close the Properties dialog box.

9. In the navigation pane, click **Software Library**.

10. In the left pane, expand **Operating Systems** and then click **Operating Systems Images**.

11. In the *Add Operating System Image Wizard*, on the *Data Source* page, right-click **Operating System Images** and choose **Add Operating System Image**.

12. In the *Open* dialog box, click the **Browse** button, browse to the **\\CServer02\REMINST\Images\ImageGroup1\install.wim** file, and then click **Open**.

13. Back in the *Add Operating System Image Wizard*, click **Next**.

14. On the *General* page, click **Next**.

15. On the *Summary* page, click **Next**.

16. Take a screenshot by pressing **Alt+Prt Scr** and then paste it into your Lab 2 worksheet file provided by pressing **Ctrl+V**.

17. Click **Close**.

18. Under *Operating Systems*, and click **Task Sequences**.

19. Right-click **Task Sequences** and choose **Create Task Sequence**.

20. In the *Create Task Sequence Wizard*, on the *Create a new task sequence* page, select **Install an existing image package** and then click **Next**.

21. On the *Specify task sequence information* page, in the *Task sequence* text box, type **Windows Server**.

22. In the *Boot image* section, click the **Browse** button. Browse to **Boot image (x64) 6.3.9600.16384 en-US** and then click **OK**. Click **Next**.

23. In the *Select an Operating System Image* dialog box, select the **Windows Server 2012 R2 SERVERSTANDARD en-US** and then click **OK**.

24. On the *Configure Network* page, click the **Join a domain** option.

25. In the *Domain* text box, type **contoso.com**.

26. In the *Account* section, click **Set**.

27. In the *Windows User Account* dialog box, in the *User name* text box, type **contoso\administrator**. In the *Password* text box and the *Confirm password* text box, type **Pa$$w0rd** and then click **OK**.

28. Back on the *Configure Network* page, click **Next**.

29. To jump to the *Summary* page, click the **Summary** option.

30. On the *Summary* page, click **Next**.

31. Take a screenshot by pressing **Alt+Prt Scr** and then paste it into your Lab 2 worksheet file provided by pressing **Ctrl+V**.

32. On the *Completion* page, click **Close**.

33. In the navigation pane, click **Assets and Compliance**.

34. In the left pane, expand **Overview** and then click **Device Collections**.

35. In the *Assets and Compliance* workspace, right-click **Device Collections** and choose **Create Device Collection**.

36. In the *Create Device Collection Wizard*, on the *General* page, in the *Name* text box, type **Server Deployment** and then click **Next**.

37. To limit the collection to another collection, click the **Browse** button. In the *Select Collection* window, click **All Systems** and then click **OK**. Click **Next**.

38. On the *Membership rules* page, click **Next**. When a message indicates that you have no membership rules, click **OK**. When you are ready to deploy, you will add the computers to the collection.

39. On the *Summary* page, click **Next**.

40. When the device collection has been created, take a screenshot by pressing **Alt+Prt Scr** and then paste it into your Lab 2 worksheet file provided by pressing **Ctrl+V**.

41. Click **Close**.

42. In the navigation pane, click **Software Library**.

43. In the *Software Library* workspace, under the *Operating Systems* node, click **Task Sequences**.

44. Right-click the **Windows Server** task sequence that you want to deploy and choose **Deploy**.

45. In the *Deploy Software Wizard*, next to the *Collection* text box, click **Browse**. In the *Select Collection* window, click **Server Deployment** and then click **OK**. When a message indicates that Server Deployment does not contain any members, click **OK**.

46. Back on the *General* page, click **Next**.

47. On the *Deployment Settings* page, for make available to the following option, select **Configuration manager clients, media, and PXE**. Click **Next**.

48. On the *Specify the schedule for the deployment* page, select the **Schedule when the deployment will become available** option and then click **Next**.

49. On the *User experience* page, you can specify what the users will see during the deployment. When done, click **Next**.

50. On the *Alerts* page, click **Next**.

51. On the *Distribution Points* page, the *Download content locally when needed by running task sequence* option is already selected for *Deployment options*. Click **Next**.

52. On the *Summary* page, click **Next**.

53. When the *Deploy Software Wizard* is complete, take a screenshot by pressing **Alt+Prt Scr** and then paste it into your Lab 2 worksheet file provided by pressing **Ctrl+V**.

54. When the Deployment has been configured, click **Close**.

Lab Challenge	Designing and Planning an Automated Server Installation Strategy (Home Security Product Project) - Continued
Overview	This Lab Challenge is a continuation of the Lab Challenge you completed in Lab 1. You will revise or update your Lab 1 plan by incorporating knowledge you gained in Lab 2. To recap, you are a new administrator for the Contoso Corporation, which is a leading producer of smart devices for the home, and you need to develop an automated installation strategy. You will read the background information for the Contoso Corporation provided in Appendix A, then read the information presented below, and then describe your solution.
Mindset	As part of a new product line consisting of home security monitoring and medical monitoring equipment for the Contoso Corporation, you need to create hundreds of servers, which will be sold as part of the product and service. Therefore, within the next three months, you will need to deploy several hundred servers for the initial launch and you will need to deploy additional servers as the product becomes more popular.
Completion time	60 minutes

The Contoso Corporation design team is close to finishing up a new product for home security monitoring and medical monitoring equipment. As a new administrator, you are called into your manager's office to discuss this exciting new project. He explains that the product is centered around a server that collects and analyzes information from wireless nodes around the house or worn by an individual. To keep track of data, the server will use Windows Internal Database (WID). As part of the rollout, hundreds of servers will need to be prepared for the product rollout and additional servers will be needed to replace sold inventory.

Your manager wants you to design a solution that can create hundreds of new servers each month. You must work with the Design team to create an automated server installation plan that will support this project. The servers will have to be tested by the quality control team before being shipped to customers.

Create a proposal that includes the following sections:

- Purpose of the Project
- Requirements of the Project
- The Proposed Solution

When writing the proposal, you must explain the reasoning behind your choices.

End of lab.

LAB 3
PLANNING AND IMPLEMENTING SERVER UPGRADE AND MIGRATION

THIS LAB CONTAINS THE FOLLOWING EXERCISES AND ACTIVITIES:

Exercise 3.1   Installing the Microsoft Application and Planning (MAP) Toolkit

Exercise 3.2   Using MAP to Perform Inventory

Exercise 3.3   Collecting Performance Metrics Using MAP

Exercise 3.4   Migrating Roles between Servers

Lab Challenge   Planning an Upgrade and Migration to Windows Server 2012 R2

BEFORE YOU BEGIN

The lab environment consists of student workstations connected to a local area network, along with a server that functions as the domain controller for a domain called contoso.com. The computers required for this lab are listed in Table 3-1.

Table 3-1
Computers required for Lab 3

Computer	Operating System	Computer Name
Server	Windows Server 2012 R2	CRWDC01
Server	Windows Server 2012 R2	CSERVER01
Server	Windows Server 2012 R2	CSERVER02

In addition to the computers, you will also need the software listed in Table 3-2 to complete Lab 3.

Table 3-2
Software required for Lab 3

Software	Location
Microsoft Application and Planning Toolkit (MAP)	\\crwdc01\software
Lab 3 student worksheet	Lab03_worksheet.docx (provided by instructor)

Working with Lab Worksheets

Each lab in this manual requires that you answer questions, shoot screen shots, and perform other activities that you will document in a worksheet named for the lab, such as Lab03_worksheet.docx. You will find these worksheets on the book companion site. It is recommended that you use a USB flash drive to store your worksheets, so you can submit them to your instructor for review. As you perform the exercises in each lab, open the appropriate worksheet file, fill in the required information, and then save the file to your flash drive.

SCENARIO

After completing this lab, you will be able to:

- Install the MAP Toolkit

- Use MAP to perform inventory and collect performance metrics

■ Migrate roles between servers

■ Plan an upgrade from Windows Server 2008 R2 to Windows Server 2012 R2

Estimated lab time: 195 minutes

Exercise 3.1	Installing the Microsoft Application and Planning (MAP) Toolkit
Overview	In this exercise, will install the MAP Toolkit.
Mindset	The MAP toolkit is a free, comprehensive agentless tool that is an inventory, assessment, and reporting tool to access the organization's environment.
Completion time	15 minutes

1. On CServer02, log on using the **contoso\administrator** account and the **Pa$$w0rd** password.

2. Open **\\crwdc01\software** and then double-click the **MapSetup** application. If you are prompted to confirm that you want to run this file, click **Run**.

3. In the *Microsoft Assessment and Planning Toolkit* wizard, on the *Welcome* page, click **Next**.

4. On the *License Agreement* page, select **I accept the terms in the License Agreement** and then click **Next**.

5. On the *Installation Folder* page, click **Next**.

6. On the *Customer Experience Improvement Program* page, select **Do not join the program at this time** and then click **Next**.

7. On the *Begin the installation* page, click **Install**.

8. When the installation is complete, click **Finish**.

9. Open the **Start menu** and click **All Programs**. Under the *Microsoft Assessment and Planning Toolkit* section, click **Microsoft Assessment and Planning Toolkit**.

10. When the Microsoft Assessment and Planning Toolkit initially opens, the *Microsoft Assessment and Planning Toolkit* dialog box opens. In the *Create an inventory database* section, in the *Name* text box, type **MAP**. Click **OK**.

11. When the Microsoft Assessment and Planning Toolkit opens, take a screenshot by pressing **Alt+Prt Scr** and then paste it into your Lab 3 worksheet file provided by pressing **Ctrl+V**.

Leave the Microsoft Assessment and Planning Toolkit open for the next exercise.

Exercise 3.2	Using MAP to Perform Inventory
Overview	In this exercise, you will use MAP to perform an inventory of your current systems.
Mindset	MAP can be used to help you determine what type of systems your organization has and if those systems can be upgraded to newer operating systems.
Completion time	15 minutes

1. On CServer02, from **Overview**, click **Perform an inventory**.

2. In the *Inventory and Assessment* wizard, on the *Inventory Scenarios* page, select **Windows computers**. Click **Next**.

3. On the *Discovery methods* page, *Active Directory Domain Services (AD DS)* is already selected. Click **Next**.

4. On the *Active Directory Credentials* page, in the *Domain* text box, type **contoso.com**. In the *Domain account* text box, type **contoso\administrator**.

5. In the *Password* text box, type **Pa$$w0rd**. Click **Next**.

6. On the *Active Directory Options* page, click **Next**.

7. On the *All Computers Credentials* page, click **Create**.

8. On the *Account Entry* page, in the *Account* name text box, type **contoso\administrator**.

9. In the *Password* and *Confirm password* text boxes, type **Pa$$w0rd**.

10. In the *Technology* section, WMI is already selected. Click **Save**.

11. Back on the *All Computers Credentials* page, click **Next**.

12. On the *Credentials Orders* page, click **Next**.

13. On the *Summary* page, click **Finish**.

14. When the *Data Collection Window* opens, and the assessment is completed, click Close.

Question 1	How many machines were discovered?

15. Wait a few minutes. Then take a screenshot of the Overview page by pressing **Alt+Prt Scr** and then paste it into your Lab 3 worksheet file provided by pressing **Ctrl+V**.

16. In the left pane, click **Server**.

Question 2	How many machines are Windows Server 2012 ready?

Leave the Microsoft Assessment and Planning Toolkit open for the next exercise.

Exercise 3.3	Collecting Performance Metrics Using MAP
Overview	In this exercise, you will use MAP to collect performance metrics for various servers.
Mindset	When you want to consolidate servers or convert physical servers to virtual servers, you need to determine how much load the current servers use. You can use MAP to collect performance metrics.
Completion time	35 minutes

1. On *CServer02*, in the left pane, click **Server Virtualization**.

2. Click **Step 2 Collect Performance data**.

3. In the *Performance Metrics Wizard*, on the *Collections Configuration* page, *Windows based machines* is already selected. Select a time 30 minutes from now. Click **Next**.

4. On the *Choose Computers* page, choose the computers from a list on the next step of the wizard is already selected. Click **Next**.

5. On the *Computer List* page, select all computers and then click **Next**.

6. On the *All Computers Credentials* page, click **Next**.

7. On the *Credentials Order* page, click **Next**.

8. On the *Summary* page, click **Finish**. You will have to wait 30 minutes for the MAP to collect the necessary information.

9. Take a screenshot of the *Server Virtualization* page by pressing **Alt+Prt Scr** and then paste it into your Lab 3 worksheet file provided by pressing **Ctrl+V**.

10. In the left pane, click **Environment**.

11. On the Environment page, click **Performance Metrics**.

12. Click **Performance Metrics Report**.

13. In the *Report Generation Status* dialog box, when the report is generated, click **Close**.

14. Take a screenshot of the *Server Virtualization* page by pressing **Alt+Prt Scr** and then paste it into your Lab 3 worksheet file provided by pressing **Ctrl+V**.

Question 3	Which program is required to read the Performance Metrics Report?

You can close the Microsoft Assessment and Planning Toolkit open for the next exercise.

Exercise 3.4	Migrating Roles Between Servers
Overview	In this exercise, you will use the Windows Server Migration Tool to migrate the DHCP server role from one server to another.
Mindset	To migrate most of the server roles from one server to another, you can use the Windows Server Migration Tool.
Completion time	70 minutes

1. Log in to CRWDC01 as **contoso\Administrator** with the password of **Pa$$w0rd**.

2. On the *Server Manager* console, click **Manage > Add Roles and Features**.

3. In the *Add Roles and Features Wizard*, click **Next**.

4. On the *Select installation type* page, click **Next**.

5. On the *Select destination server* page, click **Next**.

6. On the *Select server roles* page, click to select **DHCP** and then click **Next**.

7. In the *Add Roles and Features Wizard* dialog box, click **Add Features**.

8. Back at the *Select server roles* page, click **Next**.

9. On the *Select features* page, click **Next**.

10. On the *DHCP* page, click **Next**.

11. On the *Confirm installation selections* page, click **Install**.

12. When the installation is complete, click **Close**.

13. On CRWDC01, using *Server Manager*, open the **DHCP** console.

14. Expand the **cwdc01.contoso.com** node.

15. Right-click **IPv4** and choose **New Scope**.

16. In the *New Scope Wizard*, click **Next**.

17. In the *Name* text box, type **Main Scope**.

18. In the *Start IP address* text box, type **192.168.1.30**. In the *End IP address* text box, type **192.168.1.40**. Click **Next**.

19. On the *Add Exclusions and Delay* page, click **Next**.

20. On the *Lease Duration* page, change the lease duration to **1** day. Click **Next**.

21. On the *Configure DHCP Options* page, click **Yes, I want to configure these options now**. Click **Next**.

22. On the *Router (Default Gateway)* page, click **Next**.

23. On the *Domain Name and DNS Servers* page, in the Parent domain text box, type contoso.com. In the *IP address* text box, type **192.168.1.50** and click **Add**. Click **Next**.

24. On the *WINS Servers* page, click **Next**.

25. On the *Activate Scope* page, make sure **Yes, I want to active this scope now** and then click **Next**.

26. When the wizard is complete, click **Finish**.

27. In the *DHCP* console, right-click **rwdc01.contoso.com** and choose **Authorize**.

28. Close the **DHCP** console.

29. Log in to **CRWDC01** as **contoso\Administrator** with the password of **Pa$$w0rd**.

30. In the *Server Manager* console, click **Manage > Add Roles and Features**.

31. In the *Add Roles and Features Wizard*, click **Next**.

32. On the *Select installation type* page, click **Next**.

33. On the *Select destination server* page, click **Next**.

34. On the *Select server roles* page, click **Next**.

35. On the *Select features* page, select **Windows Server Migration Tools**. Click **Next**.

36. On the *Confirm installation selections* page, click **Install**.

37. When *Windows Server Migration Tools* is installed, click **Close**.

38. On **CServer01**, log in as **contoso\Administrator** with the password of **Pa$$w0rd**.

39. In the *Server Manager* console, click **Manage > Add Roles and Features**.

40. In the *Add Roles and Features Wizard*, click **Next**.

41. On the *Select installation type* page, click **Next.**

42. On the *Select destination server* page, click **Next**.

43. On the *Select server roles* page, click **Next**.

44. On the *Select features* page, select **Windows Server Migration Tools**. Click **Next**.

45. On the *Confirm installation selections* page, click **Install**.

46. When *Windows Server Migration Tools* is installed, click **Close**.

47. On *CRWDC01*, using *File Explorer*, open the **\\crwdc01\software** folder.

48. In the *\\crwdc01\software* folder, create a **Migrate** folder.

49. On *CRWDC01*, using *Server Manager*, open the **Services** console.

50. In the *Services* console, right-click the **DHCP server** and choose **All Tasks > Stop**.

51. Using *Server Manager*, click **Tools > Windows Server Migration Tools > Windows Server Migration Tools**.

52. From the *Windows Server Migration Tools* window, execute the following command:

   Export-SmigServerSetting -featureID DHCP -User All -Group -IPConfig –path \\crwdc01\software\migrate -Verbose

53. When you are prompted for a password, type **Pa$$w0rd** and then press **Enter**.

54. On *CServer01*, using *Server Manager*, click **Tools > Services**.

55. Right-click **DHCP Server** and choose **Stop**.

56. On *CServer01*, open **File Explorer**.

57. On *CServer01*, open the **\\crwdc01\software** folder. Then copy the **Migrate** folder to the *C* drive.

58. On *CRWDC01*, execute the **ipconfig /all** command.

Question 4	What is the MAC address for the Ethernet adapter?

59. On *CServer01*, execute the **ipconfig /all** command.

Question 5	*What is the MAC address for the Ethernet adapter?*

60. On *CServer01*, using *Server Manager*, click **Tools > Windows Server Migration Tools > Windows Server Migration Tools**.

61. From the *Windows Server Migration Tools* window, execute the following command:

    Import-SmigServerSetting -featureID DHCP -User All -Group -IPConfig all – SourcePhysicalAddress "<CRDC01 MAC address>" –TargetPhysicalAddress "<CServer01 MAC address>" –path c:\migrate -Verbose

    Whereby *<CRDC01 MAC address>* and *<CServer01 MAC address>* is recorded from the last two questions.

62. When you are prompted to provide a password, type **Pa$$w0rd** and press **Enter**.

63. On *CServer01*, on the taskbar, right-click the network notification icon and choose **Open Network and Sharing Center**.

64. In the *Network and Sharing Center*, click the **Ethernet** connection.

65. In the *Ethernet Status* dialog box, click **Properties**.

66. Double-click **Internet Protocol Version 4(TCP/IPv4)**.

67. In the *Internet Protocol Version 4 (TCP/IPv4) Properties* dialog box, change the IP address to **192.168.1.60** and the preferred DNS server to **192.168.1.50**.

68. Restart **CServer01**.

69. Log in to **CServer01** as **contoso\Administrator** with the password of **Pa$$w0rd**.

70. On *CServer01*, using the *Server Manager* console, click **Manage > Add Roles and Features**.

71. In the *Add Roles and Features Wizard*, click **Next**.

72. On the *Select installation type* page, click **Next.**

73. On the *Select destination server* page, click **Next**.

74. On the *Select server roles* page, click **Next**.

75. On the *Select features* page, select **Remote Server Administration Tools\Role Administration Tools\DHCP Server Tools** and then click **Next**.

76. On the *Confirm installation selections* page, click **Install**.

77. When the installation is complete, click **Close**.

78. On *CServer01*, using *Server Manager*, open the DHCP console and verify that the main scope is there.

79. Then, take a screenshot of the *Server Virtualization* page by pressing **Alt+Prt Scr** and then paste it into your Lab 3 worksheet file provided by pressing **Ctrl+V**.

Log off of CRWDC01 and CServer01.

Lab Challenge	Planning an Upgrade and Migration to Windows Server 2012 R2
Overview	You will read the background information for the Contoso Corporation provided in Appendix A, then read the information presented below, and then describe your solution.
Mindset	As part of a test system, you administer a test domain consisting of four servers running Windows Server 2008 R2. You have been tasked with upgrading the entire domain and all four servers to Windows Server 2012 R2, including the domain and forest functional levels.
Completion time	60 minutes

Currently, the systems are used by various groups to test various applications before they are deployed to production. Therefore, you need to devise an upgrade plan to move the domain to Windows Server 2012 R2.

Create a proposal that includes the following sections:

● Purpose of the Project

● Requirements of the Project

● The Proposed Solution

When writing the proposal, you must explain the reasoning behind your choices.

End of lab.

LAB 4
PLANNING AND DEPLOYING VIRTUAL MACHINE MANAGER SERVICES

THIS LAB CONTAINS THE FOLLOWING EXERCISES AND ACTIVITIES:

Exercise 4.1 Installing and Configuring System Center 2012 R2 Virtual Machine Manager

Exercise 4.2 Creating a VM Template and Service Template

Exercise 4.3 Creating Profiles with Virtual Machine Manager

Lab Challenge Planning a System Center 2012 R2 Virtual Machine Deployment (Data Collection and Tracking Project)

BEFORE YOU BEGIN

The lab environment consists of student workstations connected to a local area network, along with a server that functions as the domain controller for a domain called contoso.com. The computers required for this lab are listed in Table 4-1.

Table 4-1
Computers required for Lab 4

Computer	Operating System	Computer Name
Server	Windows Server 2012 R2	CRWDC01
Server	Windows Server 2012 R2	CServer01
Server	Windows Server 2012 R2	CServer02

In addition to the computers, you will also need the software listed in Table 4-2 to complete Lab 4.

Table 4-2
Software required for Lab 4

Software	Location
System Center 2012 R2 Virtual Machine Manager	\\crwdc01\software
Lab 4 student worksheet	Lab04_worksheet.docx (provided by instructor)

Working with Lab Worksheets

Each lab in this manual requires that you answer questions, shoot screen shots, and perform other activities that you will document in a worksheet named for the lab, such as Lab04_worksheet.docx. You will find these worksheets on the book companion site. It is recommended that you use a USB flash drive to store your worksheets, so you can submit them to your instructor for review. As you perform the exercises in each lab, open the appropriate worksheet file, fill in the required information, and then save the file to your flash drive.

SCENARIO

After completing this lab, you will be able to:

- Install and configure System Center2012 R2 Virtual Machine Manager

- Use VMM to create VM and service templates

- Use VMM to create and use profiles

- Plan a VM deployment

Estimated lab time: 160 minutes

Exercise 4.1	Installing and Configuring System Center 2012 R2 Virtual Machine Manager
Overview	In this exercise, you will install System Center 2012 R2 Virtual Machine Manager (VMM).
Mindset	VMM enables centralized management of virtualized workloads and allows you to manage the virtualized data center infrastructure and increase physical server utilization (including providing simple and fast consolidation of the virtual infrastructure).
Completion time	50 minutes

1. Log on to **CServer02** server using the **contoso\Administrator** account and the password **Pa$$w0rd**.

2. On *Cserver02*, using *File Explorer*, open the **\\CRWDC01\Software** folder.

3. Double-click the System Center 2012 R2 VMM ISO file and then double-click **setup.exe**.

4. When the *Microsoft System Center 2012 R2 Virtual Machine Manager* splash screen opens, click **Install**.

5. When a message displays, indicating Microsoft Visual C++ 2010 Redistributed Package was successfully installed and that the system needs to be rebooted, click **OK** and reboot CServer02.

6. Log on to **CServer02** using the **contoso\Administrator** account and the password **Pa$$w0rd**.

7. Double-click the System Center 2012 R2 VMM ISO file and double-click **setup.exe**.

8. When the *Microsoft System Center 2012 R2 Virtual Machine Manager* splash screen opens, click **Install**.

9. In the Microsoft System Center 2012 R2 Virtual Machine Manager Setup Wizard, on the *Select features to add* page, select **VMM management server** and **VMM console**. Click **Next**.

10. On the *Product registration information* page, click **Next**.

11. On the *Please read this license agreement* page, click select **I have read, understood, and agree with the terms of the license agreement** and then click **Next**.

12. On the *Customer Experience Improvement Program (CEIP)* page, select **No, I am not willing to participate** and then click **Next**.

13. On the *Installation location* page, click **Next**.

14. On the *Prerequisite* page, click **Next**.

15. On the *Database configuration* page, for the *Server* name, specify **CServer01**. *New database* is already selected and the default database is **VirtualManagerDB**. Click **Next**.

16. On the *Configure service account and distributed key management* page, *Domain account* is already selected. In the *username and domain* text box, type **contoso\administrator**. In the *Password* text box, type **Pa$$w0rd**.

Question 1	What do you need to do if you want to make VMM highly available?

17. Click **Next**.

18. On the *Port configuration* page, answer the following question and then click **Next**.

Question 2	Which port is used by the VMM console?

19. On the *Library configuration* page, *Create a new library share* is already selected. Answer the following question and then click **Next**.

Question 3	What is the location of the MSSCVMMLibrary library share?

20. On the *Installation summary* page, click **Install**. This will take a few minutes to install.

21. When VMM is installed successfully, take a screen shot of the *Microsoft System Center 2012 R2 Virtual Machine Manager Setup Wizard* by pressing **Alt+Prt Scr** and then paste it into your Lab 4 worksheet file in the page provided by pressing **Ctrl+V**.

22. Deselect **Check for the latest Virtual Machine Manager updates** and then click **Close.**

23. In the *Connect to Server* dialog box, click **Connect**. Virtual Machine Manager opens.

24. In the *Connect to Server* dialog box, select **Automatically connect with these settings** and then click **Connect**.

25. Take a screen shot of the *Virtual Machine Manager Setup Wizard* by pressing **Alt+Prt Scr** and then paste it into your Lab 4 worksheet file in the page provided by pressing **Ctrl+V.**

26. Log in to **CRWDC01** with the username of **contoso\administrator** with the password of **Pa$$w0rd**.

27. Open **Active Directory Users and Computers**. Create a domain account named **HyperVAdmin**. Make the HyperVAdmin a domain administrator.

28. Go back to **CServer02**. In the *Virtual Machine Manager*, open the Fabric workspace. Then expand the **Servers** node and click **All Hosts**.

29. Right-click **All Hosts** and choose **Add Hyper-V Hosts and Clusters**.

30. In the *Add Resource Wizard*, on the *Resource Location* page, *Windows Server computers in a trusted Active Directory domain* is already selected. Click **Next**.

31. On the *Credentials* page, *use an existing Run As account* is already selected. Click the **Browse** button.

32. In the *Select a Run As Account* dialog box, click the **Create Run As Account** button.

33. In the *Create Run As Account* dialog box, for the *Name* text box and the *User name* text box, type **contoso\hypervadmin**. For the *Password* text box and the *Confirm password* text box, type **Pa$$w0rd**. Click **OK**.

34. Back on the *Select a Run As Account* dialog box, click **OK**.

35. Back on the *Credentials* page, click **Next**.

36. On the *Discovery Scope* page, *Specify Windows Server computers by names* is already selected. In the *Computer names* text box, type **CServer02**. Click **Next**.

37. On the *Target resources* page, select **cserver02.contoso.com** and then click **Next**. When you are prompted to confirm that you want to continue, click **OK**.

38. On the *Host Settings* page, select **Reassociate this host with this VMM environment** and then click **Next**.

39. On the *Summary* page, click **Finish**.

40. When the host has been added, close the **Jobs** window.

41. Take a screen shot of the *All Hosts* node by pressing **Alt+Prt Scr** and then paste it into your Lab 4 worksheet file in the page provided by pressing **Ctrl+V**.

Leave Virtual Machine Manager open for the next exercise.

Exercise 4.2	Creating a VM Template and Service Template
Overview	In this exercise, you will create a VM template and then create a service template.
Mindset	Virtual machine templates are used to create new virtual machines and configure tiers in a service template. You can create a virtual machine template based on an existing virtual machine template or based on an existing virtual hard disk that is stored in a library. The VMM service template is a single object that contains multiple child templates, including virtual machine templates, networking configuration, load balancing, applications, and storage.
Completion time	30 minutes

1. On *Cserver02*, using *Virtual Machine Manager*, open the **Fabric** workspace.

2. On the *Home* tab, in the *Show* group, click **Fabric Resources**.

3. In the *Fabric* pane, expand the **Networking** node and then click **Logical Networks**.

4. In the *Create* group, click **Create Logical Network**. The *Create Logical Network Wizard* page opens.

5. In the *Create Logical Network Wizard* page, on the *Name* page, in the *Name* text box, type **LogicalNetwork1**. Click **Next**.

6. On the Network Site page, click Add select All Hosts.

7. Click **Insert row**. Click **Enter IP subnet**, type **192.168.1.0/24**, and then click Next.

8. On the Summary page, click **Finish**.

9. When the network is created, close the **Jobs** window.

10. Open the **Library** workspace.

11. On the Home tab, in the Create group, click **Create VM Template**.

12. In the Create VM Template Wizard, on the Select Source page, click **Use an existing VM template or a virtual hard disk stored in the library** and then click **Browse**.

13. In the Select VM Template Source dialog box, click **Blank Disk – Small.vhdx**, click **OK**, and then click **Next**.

14. On the Identity page, in the VM Template name text box, type **VMTemplate1**. Click **Next**.

15. On the Configure Hardware page, click **Memory**. Select **Dynamic memory**. For the Maximum memory, type **1024**. Click **Next**.

16. On the Configure Operating System page, answer the following question and then click **Next**.

Question 4	*What is the specified operating system?*

17. On the Summary page, click **Create**. The Jobs window opens.

18. Close the **Jobs** window. The template will appear in the Templates node.

19. Take a screen shot of the Templates node by pressing **Alt+Prt Scr** and then paste it into your Lab 4 worksheet file in the page provided by pressing **Ctrl+V**.

20. On the Library workspace, on the Home tab, in the Create group, click **Create Service Template**.

21. In the Create Service dialog box, click **Create a service template** and then click OK.

22. In the Virtual Machine Manager Service Template Designer window, in the Name text box, type **ServiceTemplate1**.

23. Click the **Blank** pattern and then click **OK**.

24. Click **Add Machine Tier**.

25. In the Create Machine Tier Template Wizard, Use a copy of an existing VM template is already selected. Click **Browse**.

26. In the Select Tier Template Source dialog box, click **VMTemplate1** and then click **OK**.

27. Back on the Select Source page, click **Next**.

28. On the Additional Properties page, click **Next**.

29. On the Summary page, click **Create**.

30. Click the **Add VM Network** button. The None VM Network box appears.

31. Click the **None** VM Network box.

32. In the bottom pane, click **Browse**.

33. In the Settings details dialog box, Use an existing VM network is already selected. Click Create **VM Network**.

34. In the Create VM Network Wizard, on the Name page, in the Name text box, type **VMNetwork1**. For the Logical network, LogicalNetwork1 is already selected. Click **Next**.

35. On the Summary page, click **Finish**.

36. On the Settings details dialog box, with use an existing VM network is selected, select **VMNetwork1** and then click **OK**.

37. Take a screen shot of the Virtual Machine Manager Service Template Designer window, by pressing **Alt+Prt Scr** and then paste it into your Lab 4 worksheet file in the page provided by pressing **Ctrl+V**.

38. Click **Save and Validate**.

39. Close the Virtual Machine Manager Service Template Designer window.

Leave Virtual Machine Manager open for the next exercise.

Exercise 4.3	Creating Profiles with Virtual Machine Manager
Overview	In this exercise, you will create different types of profiles, including an operating system profile, a hardware profile, and an application profile.
Mindset	To modularize and simplify the deployment of virtual machines, you can create profiles, which are used with a template. Since certain VM settings are common between VMs, you can use the profiles to define those settings, which can be used over and over at any time. For example, operating system profiles are used to apply a variety of settings that pertain to the operating system.
Completion time	20 minutes

1. On CServer02, using Virtual Machine Manager, open the **Library** workspace.

2. On the Home tab, in the Create group, click **Create** and then click **Guest OS Profile**.

3. In the New Guest OS Profile dialog box, on the General tab, in the Name text box, type **OS1**.

Question 5	*What is the Compatibility option set to?*

4. Click the **Guest OS Profile** tab and then configure the following settings:

   ● Operating system: Windows Server 2012 R2

   ● Admin Password: Specify the password of the local administrator password and specify the password of Pa$$w0rd.

   ● Roles: Select Web Server (IIS), IIS Management Console, Management Service, and Basic Authentication.

   ● Features: .NET Framework 3.5 (includes .NET 2.0 and 3.0), HTTP Activation, .NET Framework 4.5,

5. Click **OK** to close the New Guest OS Profile dialog box.

6. On the Library Workspace, on the Home tab, in the Create group, click **Create** and then click **Hardware Profile**.

7. In the New Hardware Profile dialog box, on the General tab, in the Name box, Type **HW1**.

Question 6	Which generation is already selected?

8. Click the Hardware Profile tab and specify the following settings.

   ● Number of processors: 2

   ● Memory: 1024 MB

9. Click **OK** to close the Hardware Profile dialog box.

10. Take a screen shot of the Profiles node by pressing **Alt+Prt Scr** and then paste it into your Lab 4 worksheet file in the page provided by pressing **Ctrl+V**.

11. Expand the **Templates** node and then click the **VM Templates** node.

12. In the Create group, click **Create VM Template**.

13. In the Create VM Template Wizard, on the Select Source page, click **Browse**.

14. In the Select VM Template Source dialog box, select **Blank Disk – Small.vhdx** and then click OK.

15. Back on the Select Source page, click **Next**.

16. On the Identity page, on the VM Template name, type **VMTemplate2** and then click **Next**.

17. On the Configure Hardware page, for the Hardware profile, select **HW1**. Click **Next**.

18. On the Configure Operating System page, for the Guest OS profile, select **OS1**. Click **Next**.

19. On the Application Configuration page, click **Next**.

20. On the SQL Server Configuration, click **Next**.

21. On the Summary page, click **Create**.

22. Close the **Jobs** window.

23. Take a screen shot of the VM Templates node by pressing **Alt+Prt Scr** and then paste it into your Lab 4 worksheet file in the page provided by pressing **Ctrl+V**.

End of exercise. Close Virtual Machine Manager.

Lab Challenge	Planning a System Center 2012 R2 Virtual Machine Deployment (Data Collection and Tracking Project)
Overview	You will read the background information for the Contoso Corporation provided in Appendix A, review the information presented in the Lab Challenge in Lab 1, read the information presented below, and then modify the solution you've provided in Lab 1.
Mindset	While planning the deployment, you determined that the hundreds of servers that you have to deploy will be virtual machines. Therefore, as an administrator, you will need to design a strategy for this task.
Completion time	60 minutes

Since these machines will be running on virtual machines, you and your team have decided to use System Center 2012 R2 Virtual Machine Manager to create, deploy, and manage the virtual machines. Therefore, you will need to modify the plan create in Lesson 1 to include using the System Center 2012 R2 Virtual Machine Manager.

Create a proposal that includes the following sections:

● Purpose of the Project

● Requirements of the Project

● The Proposed Solution

When writing the proposal, you must explain the reasoning behind your choices.

End of lab.

LAB 5
PLANNING AND IMPLEMENTING FILE AND STORAGE SERVICES

THIS LAB CONTAINS THE FOLLOWING EXERCISES AND ACTIVITIES:

Exercise 5.1 Implementing iSCSI SAN

Exercise 5.2 Planning an iSCSI Deployment

Exercise 5.3 Implementing Storage Spaces and Storage Pools

Exercise 5.4 Planning Storage Spaces and Storage Pools

Exercise 5.5 Implementing Data De-Deduplication

Lab Challenge Planning an iSCSI Storage Infrastructure (Data Collection and Tracking Project)

BEFORE YOU BEGIN

The lab environment consists of student workstations connected to a local area network, along with a server that functions as the domain controller for a domain called contoso.com. The computers required for this lab are listed in Table 5-1.

Table 5-1
Computers required for Lab 5

Computer	Operating System	Computer Name
Server	Windows Server 2012 R2	CRWDC01
Server	Windows Server 2012 R2	CServer01
Server	Windows Server 2012 R2	CServer03

In addition to the computers, you will also need the software listed in Table 5-2 to complete Lab 5.

Table 5-2
Software required for Lab 5

Software	Location
Lab 5 student worksheet	Lab05_worksheet.docx (provided by instructor)

Working with Lab Worksheets

Each lab in this manual requires that you answer questions, shoot screen shots, and perform other activities that you will document in a worksheet named for the lab, such as Lab05_worksheet.docx. You will find these worksheets on the book companion site. It is recommended that you use a USB flash drive to store your worksheets, so you can submit them to your instructor for review. As you perform the exercises in each lab, open the appropriate worksheet file, fill in the required information, and then save the file to your flash drive.

SCENARIO

After completing this lab, you will be able to:

■ Plan and implement an iSCSI implementation

■ Plan and implement a storage space and storage pool

■ Implement data de-duplication

■ Plan an iSCSI storage infrastructure

Estimated lab time: 155 minutes

Exercise 5.1	Implementing and iSCSI Target
Overview	In this exercise, you will create an iSCSI target on CServer03, which will be used by CServer01 (the iSCSI initiator). Unlike the approach used in previous courses, you will not be guided through each step. Instead, you must determine the best way to deploy the application based on the guidelines provided.
Mindset	Starting with Windows Server 2012, you can install the iSCSI Target Server role so that Windows servers can provide iSCSI storage to servers acting as iSCSI initiators or clients (known as iSCSI initiators). After you install the iSCSI Target Server role, Server Manager is used to create the volumes that will be presented to clients and to specify what servers can access the iSCSI LUNs.
Completion time	20 minutes

On CServer03, using the second hard drive (20 GB), create an ISCSI target and three virtual disks (each disk is 4 GB). Configure the ISCSI target so that is available to Cserver01.

When the three iSCSI virtual disks are created, take a screen shot of the iSCSI page by pressing **Alt+Prt Scr** and then paste it into your Lab 5 worksheet file in the page provided by pressing **Ctrl+V**.

Exercise 5.2	Planning an iSCSI Deployment
Overview	The Contoso Corporation has just purchased a new iSCSI storage area network (SAN) with multiple high-availability features. In this exercise, you will plan for an iSCSI deployment.
Mindset	The iSCSI target server included in Windows Server 2012 R2 provides boot-capable network adapters or a software loader you can use iSCSI targets to deploy diskless servers. In addition, you can use differencing disks, which can save up to 90 percent of the storage space for operating system images. The iSCSI target server also supports iSCSI initiators for Windows and non-Windows operating systems. When designing and implementing iSCSI, you need to follow iSCSI Best Practices.
Completion time	20 minutes

To accommodate all of the servers that you will be deploying, you will need a lot of disk space. Therefore, the Contoso Corporation purchased a large SAN system that supports iSCSI connections. You want to connect the SAN to your Hyper-V hosts. Therefore, to determine the best way to utilize iSCSI, answer the following questions.

Question 1	Which network technology and how would you design it so that the SAN connections are highly available while maintaining high performance?

Question 2	How would you maintain security to ensure that only the Hyper-V hosts can connect to the SAN LUNs and no other computers?

Exercise 5.3	Implementing Storage Spaces and Storage Pools
Overview	In this exercise, you will connect to an iSCSI target and create a storage space and a storage pool. You will not be guided through each step. Instead, you must determine the best way to deploy the application based on the guidelines provided.
Mindset	Storage Spaces is a feature in Windows 8.1/Windows Server 2012 R2 that allows you to combine multiple disks into a single logical volume that can use a RAID configuration to protect against one or more drive failures. When the drives are combined, Windows places them into a storage pool.
Completion time	30 minutes

CServer03 has an iSCSI target of approximately 20 GB. From CServer01, connect to the iSCSI target and create three 4 GB volumes. Using the three volumes, create a storage space (parity fault tolerance) and a pool. When finished, take a screen shot of the Storage Pools page by pressing **Alt+Prt Scr** and then paste it into your Lab 5 worksheet file in the page provided by pressing **Ctrl+V**.

Exercise 5.4	Planning Storage Spaces and Storage Pools
Overview	In this exercise, you will be provided with several scenarios and you will answer questions based on those scenarios.
Mindset	Storage spaces and storage pools allows you to combine multiple smaller drives that you might not otherwise be able to use by themselves into a larger single logical volume to give you some high availability and higher performance.
Completion time	15 minutes

Within the Contoso Corporation, you have several workstations running Windows Server 2012 R2 and those workstations are running a CAD program. The CAD files are quite large. The computers running the CAD program already have dual quad-core processors and 32 GB of memory. You determine that the disks is causing a bottleneck. How can you make the disks system faster?

Question 3	*How can you make the disks system faster while making the disks system highly available?*

Question 4	*You have six 1 TB drives in a system running Windows Server 2012 R2. One disk is used for the operating system. You want to use the additional disks for a high-performance data drive. How much space will be available if you provision the disk as parity?*

Question 5	*If you create one storage pool, how can you create the best performance storage pool? What kind of provisioning is required by the storage tiers?*

Exercise 5.5	Implementing Data De-Duplication
Overview	In this exercise, you will use data de-duplication to the new volume you just created in Exercise 5.3.
Mindset	Data de-duplication was introduced with Windows Server 2012 and reduces disk space by removing duplicate data. Data de-duplication organizes data into small chunks, identifies the duplicates, and maintains a single copy of each chunk. Data de-duplication is ideal for general shared folders, such as public and home folders, offline folders, images, software deployment shares, and VHD libraries that store VHD files.
Completion time	10 minutes

1. On CServer01, using Server Manager, click **Manage > Add Roles and Features**.

2. In the Add Roles and Features Wizard, on the Before You Begin page, click **Next**.

3. On the Installation Type page, click **Next**.

4. On the Server Selection page, click **Next**.

5. On the Server Roles, page, expand **File and Storage Services**, expand **File and iSCSI Services**, and then select **Data Deduplication**. When you are prompted to add features, click the **Add Features** button. Click **Next**.

6. On the Select Features page, click **Next**.

7. On the Confirmation page, click **Install**.

8. When the installation is complete, click **Close**.

9. Using Server Manager, click **Volumes**. Click the **E** drive.

10. Right-click the **E** drive and choose Configure Data Deduplication.

11. In the New Volume Deduplication Settings dialog box, for Data deduplication, select **General purpose file server**.

Question 6	*How old does a file have to be before it is de-duplicated?*

12. Click **OK**.

13. Right-click the **E** drive and choose **Properties**.

14. Take a screen shot of the New Volume Properties dialog box by pressing **Alt+Prt Scr** and then paste it into your Lab 5 worksheet file in the page provided by pressing **Ctrl+V**.

Lab Challenge	Planning an iSCSI Storage Infrastructure (Data Collection and Tracking Project)
Overview	You have planned the 400 or more new servers which will be deployed as virtual machines, and now the Contoso Corporation has added iSCSI SAN storage. Therefore, you will need to modify the implementation plan to accommodate the SAN storage implementation.
Mindset	By using the Hyper-V hosts combined with an iSCSI SAN, the size the data center will be significantly smaller than if you would have 400 or more physical servers with hard drives. In addition, the deployment of the servers will also be quicker and easier.
Completion time	60 minutes

During this lab challenge, you continue with the project plan that you developed in Lesson 4, now adding details about the iSCSI SAN. Remember to always plan for reliability and performance.

Create a proposal that includes the following sections:

- Purpose of the Project

- Requirements of the Project

- The Proposed Solution

When writing the proposal, you must explain the reasoning behind your choices.

End of lab.

LAB 6
DESIGNING AND MAINTAINING A DYNAMIC HOST CONFIGURATION PROTOCOL (DHCP) SOLUTION

THIS LAB CONTAINS THE FOLLOWING EXERCISES AND ACTIVITIES:

Exercise 6.1   Implementing DHCPv6

Exercise 6.2   Implementing DHCP Access Restrictions

Exercise 6.3   Maintaining a DHCP Database

Exercise 6.4   Planning DHCP Design and Maintenance

Lab Challenge   Implementing a Fault-Tolerant DHCP System (DHCP Project)

BEFORE YOU BEGIN

The lab environment consists of student workstations connected to a local area network, along with a server that functions as the domain controller for a domain called contoso.com. The computers required for this lab are listed in Table 6-1.

Table 6-1
Computers required for Lab 6

Computer	Operating System	Computer Name
Server	Windows Server 2012 R2	CRWDC01
Server	Windows Server 2012 R2	CServer01

In addition to the computers, you will also need the software listed in Table 6-2 to complete Lab 6.

Table 6-2
Software required for Lab 6

Software	Location
	\\crwdc01\software
Lab 6 student worksheet	Lab06_worksheet.docx (provided by instructor)

Working with Lab Worksheets

Each lab in this manual requires that you answer questions, shoot screen shots, and perform other activities that you will document in a worksheet named for the lab, such as Lab06_worksheet.docx. You will find these worksheets on the book companion site. It is recommended that you use a USB flash drive to store your worksheets, so you can submit them to your instructor for review. As you perform the exercises in each lab, open the appropriate worksheet file, fill in the required information, and then save the file to your flash drive.

SCENARIO

After completing this lab, you will be able to:

- Implement DHCPv6

- Create and configure an IPv6 DCHP scope

- Implement DHCP access restrictions

- Maintain a DHCP database

- Plan DHCP design and maintenance

- Implement a fault-tolerant DHCP system

Estimated lab time: 125 minutes

Exercise 6.1	Implementing DHCPv6
Overview	In this exercise, you will create a DHCP IPv6 scope with an FEC0/64 prefix. Unlike the approach used in previous courses, you will not be guided through each step. Instead, you must determine the best way to deploy the application based on the guidelines provided.
Mindset	DHCPv6 can be autoconfigured in two states: stateless and stateful. Based on router advertisements, the client will be directed to use its existing link-local addressing or to retrieve combinations of addressing and configurations from the DHCPv6 server.
Completion time	15 minutes

On CWDC01, you will create the DHCP IPv6 scope with an FEC0/64 prefix. In addition, you will exclude addresses between FEC:0000 to FEC0:0001:. If DHCP is not installed on the server, you will have to install the DHCP role. If the DHCP server is not authorized, you will have to authorize the server.

At the end of the exercise, take a screen shot of the Exclusions node by pressing **Alt+Prt Scr** and then paste it into your Lab 6 worksheet file in the page provided by pressing **Ctrl+V**.

Exercise 6.2	Implementing DHCP Access Restrictions
Overview	In this exercise, you will create a DHCP access policy that will assign specific IP configuration information to Hyper-V hosts.
Mindset	Additional management restrictions and policies can be configured to prevent, allow, and direct IP allocation based on specific criteria. By configuring policies and filtering, administrators can have more granular control over devices, virtual machines, and clients configured with a fully qualified domain name.
Completion time	15 minutes

1. On CRWDC01, open DHCP Manager, expand the DHCP server, and then expand **IPv4**.

2. Right-click **Policies** and choose **New Policy....** The DHCP Policy Configuration Wizard displays.

3. On the Policy based IP Address and Option Assignment page, in the Policy Name field, type **Policy1** and click **Next**.

4. In the Configure Conditions for the policy page, click the **Add** button.

5. In the Add/Edit Condition dialog box, from the Criteria dropdown selection, choose **MAC Address**. From the Operator dropdown selection, choose **Equals**. In the Value: text field, type **00155D**. Select the **Append wildcard (*)** check box and then click **Add**.

6. Click **OK** to close the Add/Edit Condition window and return to the DHCP Policy Configuration Wizard.

7. Click **Next**.

8. In the Configure settings for the policy page, configure the following options:

   ● 003 Router: 192.168.1.1
   ● 006 DNS Server: 192.168.1.50

   Click **Next**.

9. On the Summary page, take a screen shot of the Exclusions node by pressing **Alt+Prt Scr** and then paste it into your Lab 6 worksheet file in the page provided by pressing **Ctrl+V**.

10. Click **Finish** to return to the DHCP Manager.

11. Right-click the newly created policy and choose **Properties**.

12. In the Policy Properties dialog box, select **Set lease duration for the policy**.

Question 1	What is the default lease time?

13. Change the lease duration to 8 hours.

14. Click **OK** to close the Policy Properties dialog box.

Exercise 6.3	Maintaining a DHCP Database
Overview	In this exercise, you will back up, reconcile, and compress a DHCP database.
Mindset	Maintaining a DHCP database must be a routine and well-practiced method in order to ensure database health, safety, and security. You should know where the database and backup is located, how you can recover from a failure, and how to be proactive through maintenance.
Completion time	15 minutes

1. On CRWDC01, using the DHCP Manager console, right-click the DHCP server from the list and choose **Backup**.

2. In the Browse for Folder dialog box, answer the following question and then click **OK**.

Question 2	*What is the default backup folder location?*

3. Navigate to and select the destination path you wish to save the backup to. Click **OK**.

4. Right-click the **IPv4** node and choose **Reconcile All Scopes**.

5. In the Reconcile All Scopes dialog box, click **Verify**.

6. When the DHCP dialog box opens, indicating the database is consistent, click **OK**.

7. Close the **Reconcile All Scopes** dialog box.

8. Open Server Manager and then click **Manage > Add Roles and Features**.

9. In the Add Roles and Features Wizard, on the Before You Begin page, click **Next**.

10. On the Installation Type page, click **Next**.

11. On the Server Selection page, click **Next**.

12. On the Server Roles page, click **Next**.

13. On the Features page, select WINS Server. When you are prompted to add features, click the **Add Features** button. Click **Next**.

14. On the Confirmation page, click **Install**.

15. When the installation finishes, click **Close**.

16. Right-click the **Start** button and choose **Command Prompt (Admin)**.

17. To stop the DHCP service, execute the following command:

```
net stop dhcpserver
```

18. To compress the DHCP database, execute the following commands:

```
cd dhcp

jetpack dhcp.mdb temp.mdb
```

19. Take a screen shot of the command prompt window by pressing **Alt+Prt Scr** and then paste it into your Lab 6 worksheet file in the page provided by pressing **Ctrl+V**.

20. Close the **Command Prompt** window.

Exercise 6.4	Planning DHCP Design and Maintenance
Overview	In this written exercise, you will read the background information for the Contoso Corporation provided in Appendix A, then read the information presented below, and then describe your solution.
Mindset	Designing a DHCP solution and aligning the design with best practices will enable you to prepare for future growth as well as reliability, resilience, and high availability. A well-planned design ensures all clients will maintain network access in a secure DHCP environment.
Completion time	20 minutes

Currently, the Contoso Corporation call center has a DHCP server running Windows Server 2008 R2. For the various sites that exist, Cisco routers use a DHCP helper that relays the DHCP requests to the CRWDC01 server. Before you started with the company, the server was unavailable and the DHCP service was down for several hours while it was restored. Therefore, your manager wants to answer the following questions in hopes of creating a system that is more robust and fault-tolerant.

Question 3	What are the three methods that provide a redundant/highly available DHCP solution?

Question 4	Of these three methods, which would you recommend if you don't have many IP addresses to lease?

Question 5	You decide to use two servers to provide a fault-tolerant DHCP solution. One server is running Windows Server 2012 R2 and the other server is running Windows Server 2008 R2. Which of the three methods would you recommend?

Question 6	Over the past couple of years, there has been some confusion when assigning addresses to network devices and servers on the various subnets throughout the organization. This usually results in an IP conflict where two hosts or devices have the same IP address. What is your recommended solution to this problem?

Lab Challenge	Implementing a Fault-Tolerant DHCP System (DHCP Project)
Overview	You need to create a plan to upgrade the DHCP services to run on Windows Server 2012 R2. In addition, you need to figure out the best configuration for the DHCP server and scopes to provide high availability and robust system. You will read the background information for the Contoso Corporation provided in Appendix A, then read the information presented below, and then describe your solution.
Mindset	You are a new administrator for the Contoso Corporation, which is a leading company in producing smart devices for the home. The Contoso Corporation a DHCP cluster running on Windows Server 2008 R2 and the call center has a Windows Server 2008 R2.
Completion time	60 minutes

Create a proposal that includes the following sections:

● Purpose of the Project

● Requirements of the Project

● The Proposed Solution

When writing the proposal, you must explain the reasoning behind your choices.

End of lab.

LAB 7
DESIGNING A NAME RESOLUTION STRATEGY

THIS LAB CONTAINS THE FOLLOWING EXERCISES AND ACTIVITIES:

Exercise 7.1   Configuring DNSSEC on an Active Directory Integrated Zone

Exercise 7.2   Implementing DNS Socket Pool and DNS Cache Locking

Exercise 7.3   Creating a Single-Label DNS Name Resolution

Exercise 7.4   Planning a DNS Infrastructure and Strategy

Lab Challenge   Creating Conditional Forwarding for Contoso.com and Adatum.com

BEFORE YOU BEGIN

The lab environment consists of student workstations connected to a local area network, along with a server that functions as the domain controller for a domain called contoso.com. The computers required for this lab are listed in Table 7-1.

Table 7-1
Computers required for Lab 7

Computer	Operating System	Computer Name
Server	Windows Server 2012 R2	CRWDC01
Server	Windows Server 2012 R2	ARWDC01

In addition to the computers, you will also need the software listed in Table 7-2 to complete Lab 7.

Table 7-2
Software required for Lab 7

Software	Location
Lab 7 student worksheet	Lab07_worksheet.docx (provided by instructor)

Working with Lab Worksheets

Each lab in this manual requires that you answer questions, shoot screen shots, and perform other activities that you will document in a worksheet named for the lab, such as Lab07_worksheet.docx. You will find these worksheets on the book companion site. It is recommended that you use a USB flash drive to store your worksheets, so you can submit them to your instructor for review. As you perform the exercises in each lab, open the appropriate worksheet file, fill in the required information, and then save the file to your flash drive.

SCENARIO

After completing this lab, you will be able to:

■ Configure DNSSEC on an Active Directory integrated zone

■ Configure and implement DNS security options, including DNSSEC, DNS socket pool, and DNS cache locking

■ Create a single-label DNS name resolution

■ Planning a DNS infrastructure and strategy

■ Create a DNS GlobalNames Zone

■ Create DNS conditional forwarding

Estimated lab time: 65 minutes

Exercise 7.1	Configuring DNSSEC on an Active Directory Integrated Zone
Overview	In this exercise, you will create a domain called adatum.com and then configure DNSSEC on the adatum.com domain. Unlike the approach used in previous courses, you will not be guided through each step. Instead, you must determine the best way to perform the tasks based on the guidelines provided.
Mindset	DNSSEC is a suite of protocols defined by the Internet Engineering Task Force (IETF) for use on IP networks. DNSSEC provides DNS clients, or resolvers, with proof of identity of DNS records and verified denial of existence. DNSSEC does not provide availability or confidentiality information.
Completion time	15 minutes

After you create the adatum.com domain and configure DNSSEC, take a screen shot of the DNS Manager by pressing **Alt+Prt Scr** and then paste it into your Lab 7 worksheet file in the page provided by pressing **Ctrl+V**.

Exercise 7.2	Implementing DNS Socket Pool and DNS Cache Locking
Overview	In this exercise, you will implement the DNS socket pool (socket pool size of 2500) and DNS cache locking (100 percent). Unlike the approach used in previous courses, you will not be guided through each step. Instead, you must determine the best way to perform the tasks based on the guidelines provided.
Mindset	The DNS socket pool is a tool used to allow source port randomization for DNS queries, which reduces the chances of an attacker guessing which IP address and port (socket) the DNS traffic uses. DNS Cache Locking prevents an attacker from replacing records in the resolver cache while the Time to Live (TTL) is still in force. When cache locking is enabled, records cannot be overwritten.
Completion time	10 minutes

After you implement DNS socket pool and DNS cache locking, take a screen shot of the command prompt window by pressing **Alt+Prt Scr** and then paste it into your Lab 7 worksheet file in the page provided by pressing **Ctrl+V**.

Exercise 7.3	Creating a Single-Label DNS Name Resolution
Overview	In this exercise, you will implement the single-label DNS name resolution by using a GlobalNames zone. Unlike the approach used in previous courses, you will not be guided through each step. Instead, you must determine the best way to perform the required task based on the guidelines provided.
Mindset	In an environment where there are several DNS suffixes (such as contoso.com, adatum.com, and fabrikam.net), you can modify the suffix search order. Or you can use a GlobalNames zone within DNS, which allows a single-label name to be resolved.
Completion time	10 minutes

After you create the GlobalNames zone, take a screen shot of the DNS Manager console by pressing **Alt+Prt Scr** and then paste it into your Lab 7 worksheet file in the page provided by pressing **Ctrl+V**.

Exercise 7.4	Planning a DNS Infrastructure and Strategy
Overview	In this written exercise, you will read the background information for the Contoso Corporation provided in Appendix A, then read the information presented below, and then answer the questions.
Mindset	As an administrator for the Contoso Corporation, you need to plan and design the DNS infrastructure for internal and external DNS servers and zones. In addition, you must support DNS for both contoso.com and adatum.com forests.
Completion time	15 minutes

Recently, the Contoso Corporation has purchased Adatum Incorporated. As an administrator, you will be responsible in merging the systems used by the two organizations. You have worked with the network team to establish VPN connections between the two organizations.

Question 1	You need to locate servers and other computers from one forest to the other. What do you need to do to quickly determine the IP addresses of these servers and computers as needed?

Question 2	Adatum.com has an external DNS hosted by a web service. You would like to bring this in-house. What recommendation would you make in the placement of the DNS server that will host the external DNS for adatum.com?

Question 3	To ensure that DNS is secure, which options should be enabled in the contoso.com zone?

Lab Challenge	Creating Conditional Forwarding for Contoso.com and Adatum.com
Overview	Now that you are responsible for managing the merging of adatum.com into the contoso.com domain, you need to locate resources between forests by name. Therefore, you decide to establish DNS conditional forwarders.
Mindset	Conditional forwarding expands on the idea of forwarding, whereby you forward those queries to other DNS servers for the specified configured domain. Therefore, if you have a partner organization where you connect using a VPN tunnel, you can forward those requests to the partner's DNS when you try to access a network resource on the partner network.
Completion time	15 minutes

Write the steps you would use to set up a Windows to Go workspace.

End of lab.

LAB 8
DESIGNING AND MANAGING IP ADDRESS MANAGEMENT SOLUTION

THIS LAB CONTAINS THE FOLLOWING EXERCISES AND ACTIVITIES:

Exercise 8.1   Planning for an IPAM Implementation

Exercise 8.2   Implementing an IPAM Solution

Lab Challenge   Creating a Plan for IPAM (IPAM Project)

BEFORE YOU BEGIN

The lab environment consists of student workstations connected to a local area network, along with a server that functions as the domain controller for a domain called contoso.com. The computers required for this lab are listed in Table 8-1.

Table 8-1
Computers required for Lab 8

Computer	Operating System	Computer Name
Server	Windows Server 2012 R2	CRWDC01
Server	Windows Server 2012 R2	CServer03

In addition to the computers, you will also need the software listed in Table 8-2 to complete Lab 8.

Table 8-2
Software required for Lab 8

Software	Location
Lab 8 student worksheet	Lab08_worksheet.docx (provided by instructor)

Working with Lab Worksheets

Each lab in this manual requires that you answer questions, shoot screen shots, and perform other activities that you will document in a worksheet named for the lab, such as Lab08_worksheet.docx. You will find these worksheets on the book companion site. It is recommended that you use a USB flash drive to store your worksheets, so you can submit them to your instructor for review. As you perform the exercises in each lab, open the appropriate worksheet file, fill in the required information, and then save the file to your flash drive.

SCENARIO

After completing this lab, you will be able to:

■ Plan an IPAM implementation

■ Implement IPAM

Estimated lab time: 140 minutes

Exercise 8.1	Planning for an IPAM Implementation
Overview	In this written exercise, you will read the background information for the Contoso Corporation provided in Appendix A, then read the information presented below, and then answer the questions.
Mindset	Your manager would like to have better control over IP addressing within the organization. Therefore, he would like you to determine the best way track the usage of IP addresses.
Completion time	20 minutes

You decide to implement IP Address Management (IPAM) to help keep track of the IP addresses being used. Before you deploy IPAM, you need plan the IPAM implementation.

Question 1	Of the four servers (CRWDC01, CServer01, CServer02, and CServer03), which server would you recommend as the IPAM server? Why did you select this server?

Question 2	How many IPAM servers do you need for Contoso?

Question 3	Which topology should be used for Contoso?

Question 4	What does IPAM use to track and audit IP addresses?

Question 5	You administer a DNS server that runs on a Linux server. What do you need to do to use IPAM with the Linux server?

Question 6	How long is the forensic IP data kept?

Question 7	By looking at the Contoso Corporation, how much disk space do you think you will need in order to store the data for three years? Explain how you arrived at this figure.

Exercise 8.2	Implementing an IPAM Solution
Overview	In this exercise, you will deploy an IPAM solution on CServer03. Unlike the approach used in previous courses, you will not be guided through each step. Instead, you must determine the best way to deploy the solution based on the guidelines provided.
Mindset	IPAM is a feature within Windows Server 2012 and Window Server 2012 R2 that issued to plan, manage, track, and audit IP addresses.
Completion time	60 minutes

After the installation is complete and data has been gathered, click IP Address block and take a screen shot by pressing **Alt+Prt Scr** and then paste it into your Lab 8 worksheet file in the page provided by pressing **Ctrl+V**.

Lab Challenge	Creating a Plan for IPAM (IPAM Project)
Overview	In this written exercise, you will read the background information for the Contoso Corporation provided in Appendix A, then read the Mindset information below, and then write your plan.
Mindset	You are a new administrator for the Contoso Corporation, which is a leading company in producing smart devices for the home. To help manage the IP addresses within Contoso, you need to develop a plan for how you would implement IPAM.
Completion time	60 minutes

Create a proposal that includes the following sections:

- Purpose of the Project
- Requirements of the Project
- The Proposed Solution

When writing the proposal, you must explain the reasoning behind your choices.

End of lab.

LAB 9
DESIGNING A VPN SOLUTION

THIS LAB CONTAINS THE FOLLOWING EXERCISES AND ACTIVITIES:

Exercise 9.1   Designing a VPN Solution

Exercise 9.2   Configuring a Certificate Server

Exercise 9.3   Configuring a VPN Server

Exercise 9.4   Creating a CMAK Client Package

Exercise 9.5   Disabling Routing and Remote Access

Lab Challenge   Planning a VPN Solution (Contoso VPN Project)

BEFORE YOU BEGIN

The lab environment consists of student workstations connected to a local area network, along with a server that functions as the domain controller for a domain called contoso.com. The computers required for this lab are listed in Table 9-1.

Table 9-1
Computers required for Lab 9

Computer	Operating System	Computer Name
Server	Windows Server 2012 R2	CRWDC01
Server	Windows Server 2012 R2	CServer02
Server	Windows Server 2012 R2	CServer03

In addition to the computers, you will also need the software listed in Table 9-2 to complete Lab 9.

Table 9-2
Software required for Lab 9

Software	Location
Lab 9 student worksheet	Lab09_worksheet.docx (provided by instructor)

Working with Lab Worksheets

Each lab in this manual requires that you answer questions, shoot screen shots, and perform other activities that you will document in a worksheet named for the lab, such as Lab09_worksheet.docx. You will find these worksheets on the book companion site. It is recommended that you use a USB flash drive to store your worksheets, so you can submit them to your instructor for review. As you perform the exercises in each lab, open the appropriate worksheet file, fill in the required information, and then save the file to your flash drive.

SCENARIO

After completing this lab, you will be able to:

- Design a VPN solution

- Configure a certificate server

- Configure a VPN server

- Create a CMAK client package

- Disable Routing and Remote Access

- Plan a VPN solution

Estimated lab time: 150 minutes

Exercise 9.1	Designing a VPN Solution
Overview	In this written exercise, you will read the background information for the Contoso Corporation provided in Appendix A, then read the Mindset information below, and then answer the questions.
Mindset	VPNs link two computers or network devices through a wide-area network (WAN), such as the Internet. Because the Internet is a public network and is considered insecure, the data sent between the two computers or devices should be encapsulated and encrypted.
Completion time	15 minutes

Approximately 20 percent of your user computers are mobile computers. Your manager wants you to design a VPN solution that will allow those users to access internal resources while at home or visiting clients. While selecting the best technology to use, answer the following questions.

Question 1	Which VPN technology should you choose if the network team wants to minimize the number of open ports?

Question 2	Which ports will need to be opened if you select L2TP with IPsec and the VPN server is behind a firewall?

Question 3	Which VPN technology recommends that you deploy individual client certificates?

Question 4	Which VPN technology offers automatic VPN reconnect?

Question 5	Which versions of Windows support IKEv2?

Question 6	What is the best way to deploy VPN connections to your Windows 7, Windows 8, and Windows 8.1 machines?

Question 7	You have a mix of 32-bit and 64-bit machines running Windows 7, Windows 8, and Windows 8.1. How many CMAK packages do you need to create for the clients?

Question 8	If you select SSTP, how many certificates will you need and how should the certificate be deployed?

Question 9	Which feature or setting enables you to select which users can connect to the VPN server?

Exercise 9.2	Configuring a Certificate Server
Overview	In this exercise, you will install a certificate server on CRWDC01 so that it can be used to deploy client certificates that will be used with your VPN solution. Unlike the approach used in previous courses, you will not be guided through each step. Instead, you must determine the best way to complete the required tasks based on the guidelines provided.
Mindset	Active Directory Certificate Services (AD CS) is a server role that allows you to issue and manage digital certificates as part of a public key infrastructure (PKI). Within the PKI, the certificate authority (CA) binds a public key with respective user identities and issues digital certificates containing the public key.
Completion time	20 minutes

When the CA is configured, take a screen shot of the configured CA by pressing **Alt+Prt Scr** and then paste it into your Lab 9 worksheet file in the page provided by pressing **Ctrl+V**.

Exercise 9.3	Configuring a VPN Server
Overview	Based on the scenario for the Contoso Corporation, select a VPN technology and then install and configure the VPN server on CServer02. Unlike the approach used in previous courses, you will not be guided through each step. Instead, you must determine the best way to complete the required tasks based on the guidelines provided.
Mindset	CServer02 uses two network connections. One connection connects to the corporate network and the other connects to the perimeter network.
Completion time	25 minutes

When the VPN server is installed and configured, take a screen shot of the Routing and Remote Access window by pressing **Alt+Prt Scr** and then paste it into your Lab 9 worksheet file in the page provided by pressing **Ctrl+V**.

Exercise 9.4	Creating a CMAK Client Package
Overview	In this exercise, you will create a CMAK package that can be deployed so that users can connect to the VPN server with the technology that you selected. Then install the CMAK client on ARWDC01. Unlike the approach used in previous courses, you will not be guided through each step. Instead, you must determine the best way to complete the required tasks based on the guidelines provided.
Mindset	The Connection Manager simplifies configuring a client computer's VPN connection by using profiles with connection settings that allow local computers to connect to a remote network. When done, you then distribute the created executable file to the client computers.
Completion time	30 minutes

When the connection is complete and ready to distribute, take a screen shot of the Connection Manager Administration Kit Wizard by pressing **Alt+Prt Scr** and then paste it into your Lab 9 worksheet file in the page provided by pressing **Ctrl+V**.

Exercise 9.5	Disabling Routing and Remote Access
Overview	In this exercise, you will disable Routing and Remote Access. Unlike the approach used in previous courses, you will not be guided through each step. Instead, you must determine the best way to disable Routing and Remote Access.
Mindset	To prepare the server for the next lab, you need to reset the server by disabling Routing and Remote Access.
Completion time	10 minutes

Take a screen shot of the Routing and Remote Access page by pressing **Alt+Prt Scr** and then paste it into your Lab 9 worksheet file in the page provided by pressing **Ctrl+V**.

Lab Challenge	Planning a VPN Solution (Contoso VPN Project)
Overview	In this written exercise, you will read the background information for the Contoso Corporation provided in Appendix A, then read the information below, and then write your plan.
Mindset	You are a new administrator for the Contoso Corporation, which is a leading company in producing smart devices for the home. Now that you examined the Contoso Corporation and its infrastructure and you have researched the VPN technology you want to deploy, you will develop a plan to implement a VPN solution.
Completion time	60 minutes

When designing a VPN solution, you want to ensure that you maintain security for the corporation and the corporation resources. In addition, you have to specify all components that are needed to implement the VPN solution and how you are going to configure the clients so that they can use the VPN server.

Create a proposal that includes the following sections:

● Purpose of the Project

● Requirements of the Project

● The Proposed Solution

When writing the proposal, you must explain the reasoning behind your choices.

End of lab.

LAB 10
DESIGNING A DIRECTACCESS SOLUTION

THIS LAB CONTAINS THE FOLLOWING EXERCISES AND ACTIVITIES:

Exercise 10.1   Designing a DirectAccess Solution

Exercise 10.2   Creating a New Web Server Certificate Template

Exercise 10.3   Deploying DirectAccess

Lab Challenge   Planning a VPN Solution Revisited (Contoso VPN Project)

BEFORE YOU BEGIN

The lab environment consists of student workstations connected to a local area network, along with a server that functions as the domain controller for a domain called contoso.com. The computers required for this lab are listed in Table 10-1.

Table 10-1
Computers required for Lab 10

Computer	Operating System	Computer Name
Server	Windows Server 2012 R2	CRWDC01
Server	Windows Server 2012 R2	CServer02
Server	Windows Server 2012 R2	CServer03

In addition to the computers, you will also need the software listed in Table 10-2 to complete Lab 10.

Table 10-2
Software required for Lab 10

Software	Location
Lab 10 student worksheet	Lab10_worksheet.docx (provided by instructor)

Working with Lab Worksheets

Each lab in this manual requires that you answer questions, shoot screen shots, and perform other activities that you will document in a worksheet named for the lab, such as Lab10_worksheet.docx. You will find these worksheets on the book companion site. It is recommended that you use a USB flash drive to store your worksheets, so you can submit them to your instructor for review. As you perform the exercises in each lab, open the appropriate worksheet file, fill in the required information, and then save the file to your flash drive.

SCENARIO

After completing this lab, you will be able to:

■ Design a DirectAccess solution

■ Create a new certificate template

■ Deploy DirectAccess

Estimated lab time: 155 minutes

Exercise 10.1	Designing a DirectAccess Solution
Overview	In this written exercise, you will read the background information for the Contoso Corporation provided in Appendix A, then read the information below, and then answer the questions.
Mindset	DirectAccess is a feature that provides seamless intranet connectivity to DirectAccess client computers when they are connected to the Internet. Different from the traditional VPN connections, DirectAccess connections are automatically established and they provide always-on seamless connectivity.
Completion time	20 minutes

After discussing the VPN solution that you developed for your team, your team began a discussion about DirectAccess. Therefore, you need to decide if DirectAccess is a good fit for the Contoso Corporation.

Question 1	*What advantages does DirectAccess provide over the traditional VPN solutions available through Routing and Remote Access?*

Question 2	*Different from the traditional VPN solutions available through Routing and Remote Access, which technology must be in place to use DirectAccess?*

Question 3	*How does a client determine if it is connected through the internal network or if it is connected through the Internet?*

Question 4	*You want to place a DirectAccess server on the perimeter network. Which topology will give your company the best protection for the Contoso Corporation? Explain the logic behind your answer.*

Question 5	*Which client versions support DirectAccess?*

Question 6	*How are the clients configured to use DirectAccess?*

Question 7	*Which mechanism should be used to configure only the mobile clients to use DirectAccess?*

Question 8	*Which certificates do you need to deploy to support DirectAccess?*

Exercise 10.2	Creating a New Web Server Certificate Template
Overview	In this exercise, you will create a Web Server Certificate Template, which will be used with the DirectAccess deployment.
Mindset	For the DirectAccess deployment, you will need to deploy certificates that support server and client authentication. Therefore, you will have to create a new certificate template.
Completion time	15 minutes

1. Log in to CRWDC01 as the **Contoso\Administrator** user account with the password of **Pa$$w0rd**. The Server Manager console appears.

2. On CRWDC01, using **Server Manager**, open the **Certificate Authority**.

3. Right-click the **Certificate Templates** and choose **Manage**.

4. In the Certificate Templates Console, right-click the **Web Server** template and choose **Duplicate Template**.

5. In the Properties of New Template, select the **General** tab and then change the Template Display name to **Web Server – New**.

6. Click the **Security** tab. Make sure that domain computers can read and enroll a web server certificate.

7. Click the **Request Handling** tab, select the **Allow private key to be exported**.

8. Click the **Extensions** tab.

9. Click **Application Policies** and then click **Edit**.

10. In the Edit Application Policies Extension dialog box, click the **Add** button.

11. In the Add Application Policy dialog box, double-click **Client Authentication**. Back on the Edit Application Policies Extension dialog box, click **OK**.

12. Click **OK** to close the properties of New Template dialog box.

Question 9	Which schema version is the certificate template?

13. Close the **Certificate Templates Console**.

14. Back on the Certificate Authority console, right-click the Certificate Templates and choose **New > Certificates Template to Issue**.

15. In the Enable Certificate Templates dialog box, scroll down to and double-click **Web Server – New**.

16. Take a screen shot of the Certification Authority console by pressing **Alt+Prt Scr** and then paste it into your Lab 10 worksheet file in the page provided by pressing **Ctrl+V**.

17. Close the **Certification Authority** console.

End of Exercise.

Exercise 10.3	Deploying DirectAccess
Overview	In this exercise, you will deploy DirectAccess to CServer02, with CRWDC01/ping for the NCA.
Mindset	DirectAccess is designed for use by domain-based clients only. It cannot be used by non-domain clients. To deploy DirectAccess, you will use the Remote Access Management console.
Completion time	60 minutes

1. Log in to CRWDC01 as the **Contoso\Administrator** user account with the password of **Pa$$w0rd**. The Server Manager console appears.

2. On CRWDC01, in Server Manager, click **Tools > DNS**.

3. In the DNS Manager console, expand the **Forward Lookup Zones** and then click the **contoso.com** zone.

4. Right-click **contoso.com** and choose **New Host (A or AAAA)**.

5. In the New Host dialog box, in the Name text box, type **NLS**. In the IP address text box, type **192.168.1.70**. Select the Create associated pointer (PTR) record. Click **Add Host**.

6. Close the **DNS Manager**.

7. Log in to CServer02 as the **Contoso\Administrator** user account with the password of **Pa$$w0rd**. The Server Manager console appears.

8. On CServer02, right-click the **Start** button and choose **Run**. In the Run dialog box, in the Open text box, type **mmc** and then click **OK**.

9. In the Console1 dialog box, click **File > Add/Remove Snap-in**.

10. In the Add or Remove Snap-ins dialog box, double-click **Certificates** and then click **OK**.

11. On the Certificates snap-in page, click **Computer account** and then click **Next**.

12. On the Select Computer page, click **Finish**.

13. Back on the Add or Remove Snap-ins, click **OK**.

14. Expand the Certificates node, expand the **Personal** node, and then click the **Certificates** node.

15. Right-click the **Certificates** node and choose **All Tasks > Request New Certificate**.

16. On the Certificate Enrollment page, click **Next**.

17. On the Select Certificate Enrollment Policy page, click **Next**.

18. On the Request Certificates page, select **Web Server – New**. Then click **More information is required to enroll for this certificate. Click here to configure settings**.

19. In the Certificate Properties dialog box, in the Subject name section, for the Type, select **Common name**.

20. In the Value text box, type **CServer02.contoso.com** and then click **Add**.

21. Click **OK** to close the Certificate Properties dialog box.

22. Back on the Request Certificates page, click **Enroll**.

23. When the certificate has been enrolled, click **Finish**.

24. Right-click the **Certificates** node and choose **All Tasks > Request New Certificate**.

25. On the Certificate Enrollment page, click **Next**.

26. On the Select Certificate Enrollment Policy page, click **Next**.

27. On the Request Certificates page, select **Web Server – New**. Then click **More information is required to enroll for this certificate. Click here to configure settings**.

28. In the Certificate Properties dialog box, in the Subject name section, for the Type, select **Common name**.

29. In the Value text box, type **nls.contoso.com** and then click **Add**.

30. Click **OK** to close the Certificate Properties dialog box.

31. Back on the Request Certificates page, click **Enroll**.

32. When the certificate has been enrolled, click **Finish**.

33. In Server Manager, click **Tools > Remote Access Management**. The Remote Access Management console opens.

34. Click the **Run the Remote Access Setup Wizard** link.

35. In the Configure Remote Access Wizard, click **Deploy DirectAccess only**. The Remote Access Setup console opens.

36. Under Step 1, Remote Clients, click **Configure**. The DirectAccess Client Setup Wizard opens.

37. On the Deployment Scenario page, select **Deploy full DirectAccess for client access and remote management**. Click **Next**.

38. On the Select Groups page, select **Add**. In the Enter the object names to select text box, type **Domain Computers** and then click **OK**. Click **Next**.

39. On the Network Connectivity Assistant page, double-click a blank resource space. In the Configure Corporate Resources for NCA dialog box, change the HTTP to **PING** and then type **CRWDC01.CONTOSO.COM** in the text box. Click **Add**.

40. Back on the Network Connectivity Assistant page, click **Finish**.

41. Using Remote Access Management console, under Step 2, Remote Access Server, click **Configure**. The Remote Access Server Setup Wizard starts.

42. On the Network Topology page, click **Behind an edge device (with two network adapters)**. Then type **CServer02.contoso.com** in the text box. Click **Next**.

43. On the Network Adapters page, select **External** for the Adapter connected to the external network and select **Internal** for the Adapter connected to the internal network.

44. Click the **Browse** button. In the Windows Security dialog box, click **cserver02.contoso.com** and then click **OK**.

45. Back on the Network Adapters page, click **Next**.

46. On the Authentication page, select Use computer certificates. Click Browse. In the Windows Security dialog box, click **contoso-CRWDC01-CA** and then click **OK**.

47. Click **Finish**.

48. Under Step 3, Infrastructure Server, click Configure. The Infrastructure Server Setup Wizard starts.

49. On the Network Location Server page, click **The network location server is deployed on the Remote Access server**.

50. Click the **Browse** button. In the Windows Security dialog box, click **nsl.contoso.com** and then click **OK**.

51. Back on the Network Location Server page, click **Next**.

52. On the DNS page, click **Next**.

53. On the DNS Suffix Search List page, click **Next**.

54. On the Management page, double-click the first line of the Management Servers box to open the Add a Management Server dialog box.

55. In the Computer name text box, type **crwdc01.contoso.com** and then click **OK**.

Question 10	What other servers would you normally define as Management Servers?

56. Click **Finish**.

57. Continuing with the Remote Access Setup Configuration page, under Step 4, Application Servers, click **Configure**. The DirectAccess Application Server Setup Wizard starts.

58. On the DirectAccess Application Server Setup page, click **Finish** to accept the default option selected – Do not extend authentication.

59. At the bottom of the Remote Access Management console, click **Finish** to apply all the changes for Steps 1 through 4.

60. In the Remote Access Review dialog box, click **Apply**.

61. When the settings have been applied, click **Close**. Close the Remote Access Management Console.

62. When DirectAccess is fully deployed, take a screen shot of the Remote Access Review window by pressing **Alt+Prt Scr** and then paste it into your Lab 10 worksheet file in the page provided by pressing **Ctrl+V**.

Lab Challenge	Planning a VPN Solution Revisited (Contoso VPN Project)
Overview	In this written exercise, you will read the background information for the Contoso Corporation provided in Appendix A, then read the information below, and then write your plan.
Mindset	You are a new administrator for the Contoso Corporation, which is a leading company in producing smart devices for the home. After a meeting with your manager and your team, you decided to use DirectAccess instead of the traditional VPN solution. Therefore, you will need the previous plan from Lesson 9.
Completion time	60 minutes

Create a proposal that includes the following sections:

● Purpose of the Project

● Requirements of the Project

● The Proposed Solution

When writing the proposal, you must explain the reasoning behind your choices.

End of lab.

LAB 11
DESIGNING A WEB APPLICATION PROXY SOLUTION

THIS LAB CONTAINS THE FOLLOWING EXERCISES AND ACTIVITIES:

Exercise 11.1   Designing a Web Application Proxy Solution

Exercise 11.2   Deploying Active Directory Federation Services (AD FS)

Exercise 11.3   Configuring Web Application Proxy

Lab Challenge   Planning a VPN Solution Revisited (Contoso Web Application Proxy Project)

BEFORE YOU BEGIN

The lab environment consists of student workstations connected to a local area network, along with a server that functions as the domain controller for a domain called contoso.com. The computers required for this lab are listed in Table 11-1.

Table 11-1
Computers required for Lab 11

Computer	Operating System	Computer Name
Server	Windows Server 2012 R2	CRWDC01
Server	Windows Server 2012 R2	CServer02
Server	Windows Server 2012 R2	CServer03

In addition to the computers, you will also need the software listed in Table 11-2 to complete Lab 11.

Table 11-2
Software required for Lab 11

Software	Location
Lab 11 student worksheet	Lab11_worksheet.docx (provided by instructor)

Working with Lab Worksheets

Each lab in this manual requires that you answer questions, shoot screen shots, and perform other activities that you will document in a worksheet named for the lab, such as Lab11_worksheet.docx. You will find these worksheets on the book companion site. It is recommended that you use a USB flash drive to store your worksheets, so you can submit them to your instructor for review. As you perform the exercises in each lab, open the appropriate worksheet file, fill in the required information, and then save the file to your flash drive.

SCENARIO

After completing this lab, you will be able to:

- Design a Web Application Proxy solution

- Deploy AD FS

- Configure the Web Application Proxy

- Plan and design a Web Application Proxy solution

Estimated lab time: 145 minutes

Exercise 11.1	Designing a Web Application Proxy Solution
Overview	In this written exercise, you will read the background information for the Contoso Corporation provided in Appendix A, then read the information below, and then answer the questions.
Mindset	The Web Application Proxy is a new Remote Access Role service that provides reverse proxy functionality for web applications inside an organization network so that users can access the application externally no matter what device they are using. Since the Web Application Proxy can help publish applications securely, you should consider using Web Application Proxy with your web applications.
Completion time	20 minutes

Question 1	You want to deploy the Web Application Proxy for an external web application. Which role is required to deploy the Web Application Proxy?

Question 2	Which type of certificate is needed to protect data that is being transmitted over a network?

Question 3	Which type of authentication do you want to use if you want users to authenticate before they are redirected by a Web Authentication Proxy to the published web application?

Question 4	An application does not use claims for external users. Which type of authentication should be used when you publish an external application with the Web Authentication Proxy?

Question 5	What should you do to ensure that only authorized users access an external application published with Web Authentication Proxy using a corporate laptop?

Question 6	You are considering supporting users' personal smart phones and tablets on the corporate network. Which feature should be used to help control user access to resources?

Question 7	Three applications are published with the Web Application Proxy. To use WorkPlace-Joined devices with Web Application Proxy, which type of certificate should be deployed to the mobile devices?

Exercise 11.2	Deploying Active Directory Federation Services (AD FS)
Overview	In this exercise, you will deploy Active Directory Federation Services to CServer02, including installing the Active Directory Federation Services role and creating a standalone Federation Server. Unlike the approach used in previous courses, you will not be guided through each step. Instead, you must determine the best way to complete the requested tasks based on the guidelines provided. Hint: You will need to create a new web server certificate template so that you can deploy a web certificate to CServer02 that can be exported as a pfx file.
Mindset	AD FS role allows administrators to configure Single Sign-On (SSO) for web-based applications across a single organization or multiple organizations without requiring users to remember multiple usernames and passwords. It is also a requirement for Application Web Proxy.
Completion time	40 minutes

When AD FS is configured, take a screen shot of the Remote Access Management Console Remote Access Review window by pressing **Alt+Prt Scr** and then paste it into your Lab 11 worksheet file in the page provided by pressing **Ctrl+V**.

Exercise 11.3	Configuring Web Application Proxy
Overview	In this exercise, on CServer03, you will deploy a Web Application Proxy so that it can be used to publish external applications. Unlike the approach used in previous courses, you will not be guided through each step. Instead, you must determine the best way to complete the requested tasks based on the guidelines provided. Hint: Don't forget to deploy the Cserver02.contoso.com certificate to Cserver03.
Mindset	A reverse proxy is a proxy server that retrieves resources from servers on behalf of a client. The resources are then relayed through the proxy server to the client. As far as the client is concerned, the resources originate from the server itself. The Web Application Proxy can be used to hide the existence of the resource server and has the ability to selectively access the necessary applications on the servers inside the organization from the outside. Therefore, by using a reverse proxy, you protect applications from external threats and help protect internal resources by providing a Defense in Depth approach.
Completion time	60 minutes

When the Web Application Proxy Configuration Wizard is configured successfully, take a screen shot of the Remote Access Management Console Remote Access Review window by pressing **Alt+Prt Scr** and then paste it into your Lab 11 worksheet file in the page provided by pressing **Ctrl+V**.

Lab Challenge	Planning a Scalable Remote Access Solution (Contoso Scalable Remote Access Project)
Overview	In this written exercise, you will read the background information for the Contoso Corporation provided in Appendix A, then read the information below, and then write your plan. This project will be continued in Lab 12.
Mindset	You are a new administrator for the Contoso Corporation, which is a leading company in producing smart devices for the home. You are tasked with publishing several corporate applications over the Internet. Therefore, you will analyze the new Web Application Proxy to assess how it can be used to protect the applications.
Completion time	60 minutes

Create a proposal that includes the following sections:

- Purpose of the Project
- Requirements of the Project
- The Proposed Solution

When writing the proposal, you must explain the reasoning behind your choices.

End of lab.

LAB 12
IMPLEMENTING A SCALABLE REMOTE ACCESS SOLUTION

THIS LAB CONTAINS THE FOLLOWING EXERCISES AND ACTIVITIES:

Exercise 12.1	Designing a Scalable Remote Access Solution
Exercise 12.2	Configuring Packet Tracing
Exercise 12.3	Adding a Second Entry point for DirectAccess
Exercise 12.4	Configuring Web Application Proxy for Clustering
Lab Challenge	Planning a Scalable Remote Access Solution (Contoso Scalable Remote Access Project)

BEFORE YOU BEGIN

The lab environment consists of student workstations connected to a local area network, along with a server that functions as the domain controller for a domain called contoso.com. The computers required for this lab are listed in Table 12-1.

Table 12-1
Computers required for Lab 12

Computer	*Operating System*	*Computer Name*
Server	Windows Server 2012 R2	CRWDC01
Server	Windows Server 2012 R2	CServer02
Server	Windows Server 2012 R2	CServer03

In addition to the computers, you will also need the software listed in Table 12-2 to complete Lab 12.

Table 12-2
Software required for Lab 12

Software	Location
Lab 12 student worksheet	Lab12_worksheet.docx (provided by instructor)

Working with Lab Worksheets

Each lab in this manual requires that you answer questions, shoot screen shots, and perform other activities that you will document in a worksheet named for the lab, such as Lab12_worksheet.docx. You will find these worksheets on the book companion site. It is recommended that you use a USB flash drive to store your worksheets, so you can submit them to your instructor for review. As you perform the exercises in each lab, open the appropriate worksheet file, fill in the required information, and then save the file to your flash drive.

SCENARIO

After completing this lab, you will be able to:

- Designing a scalable remote access solution

- Enable and configure packet tracing

- Add a DirectAccess second entry point

- Configure a second Web Application Proxy

Estimated lab time: 180 minutes

Exercise 12.1	Designing a Scalable Remote Access Solution
Overview	In this written exercise, you will read the background information for the Contoso Corporation provided in Appendix A, then read the information below, and then answer the questions.
Mindset	You are almost ready to deploy DirectAccess and Web Application Proxy. Now you are going to investigate some of the advanced remote access features that come with Windows Server 2012 R2.
Completion time	20 minutes

Question 1	*On CServer10, a corporate personnel records application communicates with a SQL server. Because this application allows users to access employee information, you must ensure that the application is secure. How would you protect data that is sent over the network and how do you ensure that only the necessary traffic is sent to and from the server?*

Question 2	*You administer a server that contains highly confidential data. You want to encrypt all data that is sent to and from the server. What should you do?*

Question 3	*You administer several web servers that have some unique firewall rules. What is the easiest way to duplicate those rules to all related web servers?*

Question 4	*You administer a remote access server and some users are having trouble communicating with a web application. What can you use to look at the various packets so that you can figure out the problem?*

Question 5	*You want to make DirectAccess fault tolerant. Which options are available to you?*

Question 6	*Last week, you installed a DirectAccess infrastructure. During testing, you determined that you need to define additional application servers for DirectAccess. Which step in the DirectAccess setup should you use?*

Question 7	*You want to perform load balancing for RADIUS servers. Therefore, you install two RADIUS servers. How should you configure the RADIUS proxy servers?*

Exercise 12.2	Configuring Packet Tracing
Overview	In this exercise, you will start a packet trace for CServer02 and let it run for one minute. Then you will view the log files using the Event Viewer. Unlike the approach used in previous courses, you will not be guided through each step. Instead, you must determine the best way to perform the specified task.
Mindset	Sometimes you will encounter problems whereby the causes of the problems and the solutions to the problems might not be obvious. In some of the situations, you will need to review the packets that are being passed over the network or through a remote access server. To perform this task, you should use packet tracing or packet capturing so that you can analyze the packets.
Completion time	15 minutes

Take a screen shot of the packet tracing by pressing **Alt+Prt Scr** and then paste it into your Lab 12 worksheet file in the page provided by pressing **Ctrl+V**.

Exercise 12.3	Adding a Second Entry point for DirectAccess
Overview	In this exercise, you will enable multisite remote access and create a second DirectAccess Entry Point.
Mindset	Larger organizations will have multiple DirectAccess entry points across geographic locations. Windows 8/8.1 clients allows users to connect from the Internet to access resources within the organization network efficiently regardless of where they are located by automatically connecting to the closest DirectAccess server. If one of the access points is not available, the clients will failover to another entry point.
Completion time	60 minutes

1. Log in to CServer03 as **contoso\administrator** with the password of **Pa$$w0rd**.

2. Right-click the network status icon on the task bar and click **Open Network and Sharing Center**.

3. In the Network and Sharing Center window, click **Change Adapter settings**.

4. Right-click the first Ethernet connection, click **rename**, and then type **Internal**.

5. Right-click the second Ethernet connection, click **rename**, and then type **External**.

6. Right-click the External connection and choose **Properties**.

7. In the External Properties dialog box, double-click **Internet Protocol Version 4 (TCP/IPv4)**.

8. In the Internet Protocol Version 4 (TCP/IPv4) Properties dialog box, type the following:

   IP address: **192.168.2.2**

   Subnet mask: **255.255.255.0**

   Click **OK**.

9. To close the External Properties dialog box, click **OK**.

10. Log in to CRWDC01 as **contoso\administrator** with the password of **Pa$$w0rd**.

11. On CRWDC01, in Server Manager, click **Tools > DNS**.

12. In the DNS Manager console, expand the **Forward Lookup Zones** and then click the **contoso.com** zone.

13. Right-click **contoso.com** and choose **New Host (A or AAAA)**.

14. In the New Host dialog box, in the Name text box, type **NLS**. In the IP address text box, type **192.168.1.80**. Select **Create associated pointer (PTR) record**. Click **Add Host**.

15. Repeat the process and add a host record for **NLS.contoso.com** that points to **192.168.1.80**.

Question 8	What does the two DNS entries that use the same name do for the servers?

16. Close **DNS Manager**.

17. If you are not logged into Cserver02, log in to **CServer02** as **contoso\administrator** with the password of **Pa$$w0rd**.

18. Right-click the **Start** button and choose **Run**. In the Run dialog box, in the Open text box, type **mmc** and then click **OK**.

19. In the Console1 dialog box, click **File > Add/Remove Snap-in**.

20. In the Add or Remove Snap-ins dialog box, double-click **Certificates** and then click **OK**.

21. On the Certificates snap-in page, click **Computer account** and then click **Next**.

22. On the Select Computer page, click **Finish**.

23. Back on the Add or Remove Snap-ins, click **OK**.

24. Expand the **Certificates** node, expand the **Personal** node, and then click the **Certificates** node.

25. Right-click the **nls.contoso.com** certificate and choose **All Tasks > Export**.

26. In the Certificate Export Wizard, on the Welcome page, click **Next**.

27. On the Export Private Key, select **Yes, export the private key**. Click **Next**.

28. On the Export File Format, select **Export all extended properties**. Click **Next**.

29. On the Security page, select **Password**. Then in the Password text box and the Confirm password text box, type **Pa$$w0rd**. Click **Next**.

30. On the File to Export page, type **\\crwdc01\software\nls.pfx**.

31. When the wizard is complete, click **Finish**.

32. When the export is successful, click **OK**.

33. On CServer03, using the Console1 with the Certificates snap-in, right-click the **Certificates** node and choose **All Tasks > Import**.

34. In the Certificate Import Wizard, on the Welcome page, click **Next**.

35. On the File to Import page, in the File name text box, type **\\crwdc01\software\nls.pfx** and then click **Next**.

36. On the Private key protection page, in the Password text box, type **Pa$$w0rd**. Click **Next**.

37. On the Certificate Store page, click **Next**.

38. When the wizard is complete, click **Finish**.

39. When the import was successful, click **OK**.

40. Right-click the **Certificates** node and choose **All Tasks > Request New Certificate**.

41. In the Certificate Enrollment wizard, on the Before You Begin page, click **Next**.

42. On the Select Certificate Enrollment Policy page, click **Next**.

43. On the Request Certificates page, select **Web Server – New**. Then click **More information is required to enroll for this certificate. Click here to configure settings.**

44. In the Certificate Properties dialog box, in the Subject name section, for the Type, select **Common name**.

45. In the Value text box, type **CServer03.contoso.com** and then click **Add**. Click **OK** to close the Certificate Properties dialog box.

46. Back on the Request Certificates page, click **Enroll**.

47. When the certificate has been enrolled, click **Finish**.

48. On CServer02, using Server Manager, click **Tools > Remote Access Management**.

49. Under Tasks, click **Enable Multisite**.

50. In the Enable Multisite Deployment wizard, on the Before You Begin page, click **Next**.

51. On the Deployment Name page, the default name of the Multisite deployment name is Enterprise. In the First entry point name text box, type **Corporate**. Click **Next**.

52. On the Entry Point Selection page, Assign entry points automatically, and allow clients to select manually is selected. Click **Next**.

53. On the Global Load Balancing Settings page, click **Next**.

54. On the Client Support page, Limit access to client computers running Windows 8 or a later operating system option is selected. Click **Next**.

55. On the Summary page, take a screen shot of the Enable Multisite Deployment window by pressing **Alt+Prt Scr** and then paste it into your Lab 12 worksheet file in the page provided by pressing **Ctrl+V**.

56. Click **Commit**.

57. When the configuration has been applied, click **Close**.

58. Click **Close** to close the Enable Multisite Deployment wizard.

59. On CServer02, using Remote Access Management, under the Tasks pane, click **Add an Entry Point**.

60. In the Add an Entry Point wizard, on the Entry Point Details page, in the Remote Access server and Entry point name text boxes, type **cserver03.contoso.com**. Click **Next**.

61. On the Network Topology page, select **Behind an edge device (with two network adapters)** and then click **Next**.

62. On the Network name or IP address page, in the text box, type **cserver03.contoso.com**. Click **Next**.

63. On the Network Adapters page, click the **Browse** button and select the **cserver03.contoso.com** certificate. Click **OK**. Click **Next**.

64. On the Prefix Configuration page, click **Next**.

65. On the Client Support page, click **Next**.

66. On the Server GPO Settings page, click **Next**.

67. On the Network Location Server page, use the **Browse** button, select the **NLS.contoso.com** certificate, and then click **OK**. Click **Next**.

68. On the Summary page, click **Commit**. When the changes have been saved, click **Close**.

69. Click **Close** to close the Add an Entry point wizard.

70. On the Summary page, take a screen shot of the Remote Access Setup window by pressing **Alt+Prt Scr** and then paste it into your Lab 12 worksheet file in the page provided by pressing **Ctrl+V**.

Exercise 12.4	Configuring Web Application Proxy For Clustering
Overview	In this exercise, you will configure a second Web Application Proxy on CServer01.
Mindset	The Web Application Proxy preauthenticates access to web applications using AD FS and functions as an AD FS proxy. In addition, you can install multiple AD FS proxy servers to form a cluster.
Completion time	25 minutes

1. Log in to CServer03 as **contoso\administrator** with the password of **Pa$$w0rd**.

2. On Cserver03, open the MMC console by executing the **mmc** command.

3. Click **File > Add/Remove Snap-in**. Double-click **Certificates**. In the Certificates snap-in dialog box, select **Computer account** and then click **Finish**.

4. On the Select Computers page, with Local Computer selected, click **Finish**.

5. Right-click the **Certificates\Personal\Certificates** node and choose **All Tasks > Import**.

6. In the Welcome to the Certificate Import Wizard, click **Next**.

7. On the File to Import page, type **\\crwdc01\software\cserver02.pfx**.

8. On the Private key protection page, in the Password text box, type **Pa$$w0rd**. Click **Next**.

9. On the Certificate Store page, click **Next**.

10. On the Completing the Certificate Import Wizard page, click **Finish**.

11. When the Certificate Import Wizard is successful, click **OK**.

12. On CServer01 using Server Manager, click **Manage > Add roles and features**.

13. On the Before you begin page, click **Next**.

14. Select **Role-based or feature-based installation** and then click **Next**.

15. On the Server select page, click **Next**.

16. On the Select server roles page, select **Remote Access** and then click **Next**.

17. Click **Next** twice.

18. In the Select role page, select **Web Application Proxy**, click **Add Features**, and then click **Next**.

19. In the Confirm installation selections dialog box, click **Install**.

20. When the installation is complete, click the **Open the Web Application Proxy Wizard** link.

21. On the Welcome page, click **Next**.

22. On the Federation Server page, for the Federation service name, type **cserver02.contoso.com**.

23. For the Username, type **contoso\administrator**, and for the password, type **Pa$$w0rd**. Click **Next**.

24. On the AD FS Proxy Certificate page, select the **CServer02.contoso.com** certificate and click **Next**.

25. On the Confirmation page, click **Configure**.

26. On the Results page, click **Close**.

27. On the Summary page, take a screen shot of the Remote Access Management Console window showing the Web Application Proxy and the two cluster servers by pressing **Alt+Prt Scr** and then paste it into your Lab 12 worksheet file in the page provided by pressing **Ctrl+V**.

Lab Challenge	Planning a Scalable Remote Access Solution (Contoso Scalable Remote Access Project).
Overview	In this written exercise, you will read the background information for the Contoso Corporation provided in Appendix A, then read the information below, and then write your plan. This project is a continuation of Lab 11. Apply the knowledge you have gained in Lab 12 to revise the plan you developed in Lab 11.
Mindset	You are a new administrator for the Contoso Corporation, which is a leading company in producing smart devices for the home. You are tasked with publishing several corporate applications over the Internet. Therefore, you will analyze the new Web Application Proxy to assess how it can be used to protect the applications.
Completion time	30 minutes

Create a proposal that includes the following sections:

● Purpose of the Project

● Requirements of the Project

● The Proposed Solution

When writing the proposal, you must explain the reasoning behind your choices.

End of lab.

LAB 13
DESIGNING AND IMPLEMENTING A NETWORK PROTECTION SOLUTION

THIS LAB CONTAINS THE FOLLOWING EXERCISES AND ACTIVITIES:

Exercise 13.1   Designing Network Access Protection

Exercise 13.2   Installing a Network Policy Server

Exercise 13.3   Configuring NAP Enforcement for IPsec

Lab Challenge   Planning a Windows Update and Anti-virus Solution (Contoso Client
                      Security Project)

BEFORE YOU BEGIN

The lab environment consists of student workstations connected to a local area network, along
with a server that functions as the domain controller for a domain called contoso.com. The
computers required for this lab are listed in Table 13-1.

Table 13-1
Computers required for Lab 13

Computer	Operating System	Computer Name
Server	Windows Server 2012 R2	CRWDC01
Server	Windows Server 2012 R2	CServer01

In addition to the computers, you will also need the software listed in Table 13-2 to complete Lab 13.

Table 13-2
Software required for Lab 13

Software	Location
Lab 13 student worksheet	Lab13_worksheet.docx (provided by instructor)

Working with Lab Worksheets

Each lab in this manual requires that you answer questions, shoot screen shots, and perform other activities that you will document in a worksheet named for the lab, such as Lab13_worksheet.docx. You will find these worksheets on the book companion site. It is recommended that you use a USB flash drive to store your worksheets, so you can submit them to your instructor for review. As you perform the exercises in each lab, open the appropriate worksheet file, fill in the required information, and then save the file to your flash drive.

SCENARIO

After completing this lab, you will be able to:

- Design Network Access Protection

- Install and configure Network Access Protection

- Configure NAP enforcement for IPsec

- Plan a Windows update and anti-virus solution

Estimated lab time: 160 minutes

Exercise 13.1	Designing Network Access Protection
Overview	In this written exercise, you will read the background information for the Contoso Corporation provided in Appendix A, then read the information below, and then answer the questions.
Mindset	To keep internal resources secure, you need to ensure that your systems have the newest software updates and that you have an up-to-date anti-virus program.
Completion time	20 minutes

Question 1	Which NAP enforcement method is the easiest for a user to bypass and why?

Question 2	If you use DirectAccess, which type of NAP enforcement should you use?

Question 3	What type of NAP enforcement should be used when you want to ensure that all clients connected the internal corporate network?

Question 4	How many HRA servers will you need for the Contoso Corporation?

Question 5	What should you do when you have a large amount of NPS requests that a single server cannot handle by itself?

Question 6	Which Contoso servers could be identified as a remediation server?

Exercise 13.2	Installing a Network Policy Server
Overview	In this exercise, you will install Network Policy Server on CServer01. Unlike the approach used in previous courses, you will not be guided through each step. Instead, you must determine the best way to complete the task based on the guidelines provided. Hint: You will need to deploy a certificate for CServer01.
Mindset	Network Access Protection (NAP) is Microsoft's solution for controlling network access for computers based on the health of the host, such as if it is the newest security patches and a current anti-virus/anti-malware software package. NAP IPsec provides the strongest and most flexible method for maintaining client computer compliance with network health requirements.
Completion time	20 minutes

When the installation is complete, take a screen shot of the of the Add Roles and Features Wizard by pressing **Alt+Prt Scr** and then paste it into your Lab 13 worksheet file in the page provided by pressing **Ctrl+V**.

Exercise 13.3	Configuring the NAP Policies for IPsec
Overview	In this exercise, you will create a NAP policy for IPsec on a NAP server and configure a GPO to support IPsec for NAP.
Mindset	NAP IPsec provides the strongest and most flexible method for maintaining client computer compliance with network health requirements. It provides secure communications with compliant clients based on IP address or port number.
Completion time	30 minutes

1. If you are not logged into CServer01, log in as **contoso\administrators** with the password of **Pa$$0wrd**.

2. On CServer01, using Server Manager, click **Tools > Network Policy Server**. The Network Policy Server console opens.

3. In the main pane, click **Configure NAP** to start the Configure NAP Wizard.

4. For the Network connection method option, select **IPsec with Health Registration Authority (HRA)**.

Question 7	*What is the default policy name?*

5. Click **Next**.

6. On the Specify NAP Enforcement Servers Running HRA page, for the RADIUS clients, click **Add**.

7. In the New RADIUS Client dialog box, type **CServer01**. In the Address (IP or DNS) text box, type **192.168.1.60**.

8. In the Shared secret and Confirm shared secret text boxes, type **Pa$$w0rd**. Click **OK**.

9. Back on the Specify NAP Enforcement Servers Running HRA page, click **Next**.

10. On the Configure Machine Groups page, click **Add**. In the Select Group dialog box, in the Enter the object name to select text box, type **Domain Guests**. Click **OK**.

11. Back on the Configure Machine Groups page, click **Next**.

12. On the Define NAP Health Policy page, Windows Security Health Validator and Enable auto-remediation of client computers options are already selected. Click **Next**.

13. On the Completing NAP Enforcement Policy and RADIUS Client Configuration page, click **Finish**.

14. Expand the **Policies** node and click **Network Policies**. Take a screen shot of the of the Network Policies by pressing **Alt+Prt Scr** and then paste it into your Lab 13 worksheet file in the page provided by pressing **Ctrl+V**.

15. Log in to CRWDC01 as **contoso\administrators** with the password of **Pa$$0wrd**.

16. On CRWDC01, using Server Manager, click **Tools > Group Policy Management**.

17. Navigate to the **Forest:contoso.com\Domains\contoso.com** node and right-click **Group Policy Objects** and choose click **New**.

18. In the New GPO dialog box, in the Name text box, type **IPsec** and then click **OK**.

19. Right-click the **IPsec** policy and choose **Edit**.

20. Navigate to the **Computer Configuration\Policies\Windows Settings\Security Settings\Network Access Protection\NAP Client Configuration\Health Registration Settings\Trusted Server Groups** node.

21. Right-click the **Trusted Server Groups** node and choose **New**.

22. In the New Trusted Server Group dialog box, in the Group Name text box, type **IPsec Servers**. Click **Next**.

23. On the Add Servers page, in the Add URLS of the health registration authority that you want the client to trust text box, type **https://cserver01.contoso.com /domainhra/hcsrvext.dll** and click **Add**. Click **Next**.

24. On the Completing the new trusted server group wizard page, click **Finish**.

25. Take a screen shot of the of the Trusted Server Groups by pressing **Alt+Prt Scr** and then paste it into your Lab 13 worksheet file in the page provided by pressing **Ctrl+V**.

26. Navigate to the **Computer Configuration\Policies\Windows Settings\Security Settings\Network Access Protection\NAP Client Configuration\Enforcement Clients** node. Then double-click **IPsec Relying Party**.

27. In the IPsec Relying Party Properties dialog box, select **Enable this enforcement client**. Click **OK**.

28. Navigate to **Computer Configuration/Policies/Windows Settings/Security Settings/System Services** node.

29. In the details pane, double-click **Network Access Protection Agent**.

30. In the Network Access Protection Agent Properties dialog box, select the **Define this policy setting** check box, choose **Automatic**, and then click **OK**.

31. Navigate to the **Computer Configuration\Policies\Administrative Templates\Windows Components\Security Center** node.

32. Double-click the **Turn on Security Center (Domain PCs only)**.

33. In the Turn on Security Center (Domain PCs only) dialog box, select **Enable** and then click **OK**.

34. Close the **Group Policy Management Editor**.

35. On the Group Policy Management console, with the IPsec policy selected, click the **Settings** tab. Click **show all**.

36. Take a screen shot of the IPsec policy by pressing **Alt+Prt Scr** and then paste it into your Lab 13 worksheet file in the page provided by pressing **Ctrl+V**.

37. Close the **Group Policy Management** console.

Lab Challenge	Planning a Windows Update and Anti-Virus Solution (Contoso Client Security Project)
Overview	In this written exercise, you will read the background information for the Contoso Corporation provided in Appendix A, then read the information below, and then write your plan.
Mindset	You are a new administrator for the Contoso Corporation, which is a leading company in producing smart devices for the home. Your manager has tasked you with devising a plan that ensures all systems are kept up-to-date with Windows updates and Office updates and as well as a current anti-virus package. Hint: Besides installing NAP servers and determining the NAP enforcement method, you also need to determine how you are going to deploy the updates and anti-virus software.
Completion time	90 minutes

Create a proposal that includes the following sections:

● Purpose of the Project

● Requirements of the Project

● The Proposed Solution

When writing the proposal, you must explain the reasoning behind your choices.

End of lab.

LAB 14
DESIGNING A FOREST AND DOMAIN INFRASTRUCTURE

THIS LAB CONTAINS THE FOLLOWING EXERCISES AND ACTIVITIES:

Exercise 14.1   Designing the Forest and Domain Infrastructure

Exercise 14.2   Upgrading a Domain to Windows Server 2012 R2

Lab Challenge   Planning a Forest and Domain Infrastructure (Contoso Forest and Domain Infrastructure Project)

BEFORE YOU BEGIN

The lab environment consists of student workstations connected to a local area network, along with a server that functions as the domain controller for a domain called contoso.com. The computers required for this lab are listed in Table 14-1.

Table 14-1
Computers required for Lab 14

Computer	Operating System	Computer Name
Server	Windows Server 2012 R2	ARWDC01

In addition to the computers, you will also need the software listed in Table 14-2 to complete Lab 14.

Table 14-2
Software required for Lab 14

Software	Location
Lab 14 student worksheet	Lab14_worksheet.docx (provided by instructor)

Working with Lab Worksheets

Each lab in this manual requires that you answer questions, shoot screen shots, and perform other activities that you will document in a worksheet named for the lab, such as Lab14_worksheet.docx. You will find these worksheets on the book companion site. It is recommended that you use a USB flash drive to store your worksheets, so you can submit them to your instructor for review. As you perform the exercises in each lab, open the appropriate worksheet file, fill in the required information, and then save the file to your flash drive.

SCENARIO

After completing this lab, you will be able to:

- Design a forest and domain infrastructure

- Upgrade a domain to Windows Server 2012 R2

- Plan a forest and domain infrastructure

Estimated lab time: 140 minutes

Exercise 14.1	Designing the Forest and Domain Infrastructure
Overview	In this written exercise, you will read the background information for the Contoso Corporation provided in Appendix A, then read the information below, and then answer the questions.
Mindset	While you are a relatively new administrator at the Contoso Corporation, you have now been there long enough to understand how Active Directory was designed and how your company interfaces with Active Directory. You now need to look at the Active Directory forest and domain and figure how it can be optimized for your company.
Completion time	40 minutes

Question 1	When you first started with the company, your manage told you that he wanted you to look at all aspects of the IT department and determine the best way to optimize the network infrastructure, including Active Directory. What should be your first step in designing a forest and domain structure and before any restructuring is done? Explain how you would accomplish this step for the Contoso Corporation.
Question 2	Looking at the Contoso Corporation, including the purchase of Adatum Incorporated, would you recommend keeping the two forests or would you recommend merging the two forests into one? Explain your answer.
Question 3	How would you perform administrative isolation and resource separation if the Contoso Corporation decided to do some top-secret work for the military?
Question 4	Looking at the Contoso Corporation documentation, what type of forest model is used by the Contoso Corporation?
Question 5	Looking at the documentation for the Contoso Corporation, what is the primary forest root domain?
Question 6	How many domains would you recommend for the Contoso Corporation?

Question 7	While you merge the resources between the Contoso Corporation and Adatum Incorporated, what kind of trust should you set up between the two forests?

Question 8	If you purchase a company that is a UNIX shop, what kind of trust would you configure between the contoso.com domain and the newly purchased company?

Question 9	You administer a large forest with 22 domains. You notice that authentication is slow between some of the domains. What can you do to speed up the authentication?

Question 10	For the Contoso Corporation, what is the highest domain functional level that you can use? Explain your answer.

Question 11	For the Contoso Corporation, which migration path would you use to upgrade the domain to Windows Server 2012 R2? Explain your answer.

Question 12	You administer a forest/domain that has several domain controllers running Windows Server 2008 R2. What is the first step you would need to perform before you can add the first server running Windows Server 2012 R2 to the domain?

Question 13	You administer a forest/domain that has several domain controllers running Windows Server 2008 R2. What is the first step you would need to perform before you can add the first domain controller running Windows Server 2012 R2 to the domain?

Question 14	You decide to use Azure to host several servers for a new corporate application. How should you interface the servers so that the application can access the newest Active Directory information?

Exercise 14.2	Upgrading a Domain to Windows Server 2012 R2
Overview	In this written exercise, you will upgrade Windows Server 2008 R2 to Windows Server 2012 R2 and update the forest and domain functional level to Windows Server 2012 R2. The installation files for Windows Server 2012 R2 are in the \\arwdc01\software\Win2012R2 folder. Unlike the approach used in previous courses, you will not be guided through each step. Instead, you must determine the best way to perform the required tasks based on the guidelines provided.
Mindset	Upgrading Windows Server 2008 R2 or Windows Server 2012 domain to Windows Server 2012 R2 domain is basically a matter of introducing a Windows Server 2012 R2 domain controller onto the network. To prepare the forest and the domain for the upgrade, you must modify the schema of your existing Active Directory installation. Then you can upgrade one of the domain controllers to Windows Server 2012 R2 or install a new Windows Server 2012 R2 domain controller.
Completion time	40 minutes

After the system has been upgraded, take a screen shot of the Exclusions node by pressing **Alt+Prt Scr** and then paste it into your Lab 14 worksheet file in the page provided by pressing **Ctrl+V**.

At the end of the exercise, take a screen shot of the forest level being successful raised by pressing **Alt+Prt Scr** and then paste it into your Lab 14 worksheet file in the page provided by pressing **Ctrl+V**.

Lab Challenge	Planning a Forest and Domain Infrastructure (Contoso Forest and Domain Infrastructure Project)
Overview	In this written exercise, you will read the background information for the Contoso Corporation provided in Appendix A, then read the information below, and then write your plan. This project will continue in Lab 15.
Mindset	You are a new administrator for the Contoso Corporation, which is a leading company in producing smart devices for the home. As a team lead for the Windows Server team, you need to develop a plan to update the Contoso Forest and Domain Infrastructure to Windows Server 2012 R2. In addition, you need assess the best way to reorganize the forest and domain structure. Therefore, you need to determine what needs to be reorganized and how you would reorganize the forest and domain.
Completion time	60 minutes

Create a proposal that includes the following sections:

- Purpose of the Project

- Requirements of the Project

- The Proposed Solution

When writing the proposal, you must explain the reasoning behind your choices.

End of lab.

LAB 15
IMPLEMENTING A FOREST AND DOMAIN INFRASTRUCTURE

BEFORE YOU BEGIN

The lab environment consists of student workstations connected to a local area network, along with a server that functions as the domain controller for a domain called contoso.com. The computers required for this lab are listed in Table 15-1.

Table 15-1
Computers required for Lab 15

Computer	Operating System	Computer Name
Server	Windows Server 2008 R2	CRWDC01
		ARWDC01

In addition to the computers, you will also need the software listed in Table 15-2 to complete Lab 15.

Table 15-2
Software required for Lab 15

Software	Location
Windows Server 2012 R2 Installation Disk	\\arwdc01\software
SQL Server 2012 Installation files	\\arwdc01\software\SQL2012
Active Directory Migration Tool Installation Wizard (admtsetup32.exe)	\\arwdc01\software
Lab 15 student worksheet	Lab15_worksheet.docx (provided by instructor)

Working with Lab Worksheets

Each lab in this manual requires that you answer questions, shoot screen shots, and perform other activities that you will document in a worksheet named for the lab, such as Lab15_worksheet.docx. You will find these worksheets on the book companion site. It is recommended that you use a USB flash drive to store your worksheets, so you can submit them to your instructor for review. As you perform the exercises in each lab, open the appropriate worksheet file, fill in the required information, and then save the file to your flash drive.

SCENARIO

After completing this lab, you will be able to:

- Rename a domain

- Create a trust relationship between two forests

- Install ADMT

- Migrate a user from one forest/domain to another

- Plan a forest and domain infrastructure

Estimated lab time: 230 minutes

Exercise 15.1	Renaming a Domain
Overview	In this exercise, you will rename the adatum.com to cadatum.com.
Mindset	The renaming of a domain is one of the more serious changes that you can do with Active Directory. Since Active Directory is used by users, computers, and applications for authentication and authorization, when you rename a domain, you are changing the entire networking environment. Therefore, you will need to plan out the renaming of a domain and then implement the change during the off hours.
Completion time	40 minutes

1. On ARWDC01, log on using the **adatum\administrator** account and the **Pa$$w0rd** password.

Question 1	*What should you do before you perform any major domain or forest changes?*

2. Using Server Manager, open **DNS server**.

3. Right-click the **Forward Lookup Zones** and choose **New Zone**.

4. In the New Zone Wizard, click **Next**.

5. On the Zone Type page, click **Next**.

6. On the Active Directory Zone Replication Scope page, click **Next**.

7. On the Zone Name page, in the Zone name text box, type **cadatum.com** and then click **Next**.

8. On the Dynamic Update page, click **Next**.

9. When the wizard is complete, click **Finish**.

10. Right-click the **Start** button and choose **Command Prompt (Admin)**.

11. To create the domainlist.xml file, execute the **rendom.exe /list** command.

12. Using File Explorer, open the **C:\Windows\System32** folder. Then right-click the **domainlist.xml** file and choose **Edit**.

13. In the xml file, make the following changes and then save the xml file:

    - <DNSname>ForetDNSZones.adatum.com</DNSname> to <DNSname>ForetDNSZones.cadatum.com</DNSname>

- <DNSname>DomainDNSZones.adatum.com>/DNSname> to
  <DNSname>DomainDNSZones.cadatum.com>/DNSname>

- <DNSname>adatum.com<DNSname> to <DNSname>cadatum.com<DNSname>

- <NetBiosName>ADATUM</NetBiosName> to <NetBiosName>CADATUM</NetBiosName>

14. To create a dclist.xml file, execute the **random.exe /upload** command.

15. Push domain rename instructions by executing the following command:

    repadmin /syncall /d /e /P /q arwdc01

16. Verify that the domain controllers are ready by executing the **rendom /prepare** command.

17. To perform the renaming of the domains, execute the **rendom /execute** command.

18. When a message appears, indicating that Directory Service is shutting down, click **Close**. Windows will reboot after a minute or so.

19. On ARWDC01, log on using the **cadatum\administrator** account and the **Pa$$w0rd** password.

20. Right-click the **Start** button and choose **Command Prompt (Admin)**.

21. At the command prompt, execute the rendom /end command.

22. Using Server Manager, open **Active Directory Domains and Trusts**.

23. At the end of the exercise, take a screen shot of the Active Directory Domains and Trusts window by pressing **Alt+Prt Scr** and then paste it into your Lab 15 worksheet file in the page provided by pressing **Ctrl+V**.

24. Right-click the **Start** button and choose **System**.

25. In the System window, click **Change settings**.

26. In the System Properties dialog box, click **Change**.

27. In the Computer Name/Domain Changes dialog box, click **OK**.

28. In the Computer Name/Domain Changes dialog box, click **More**.

29. In the Primary DNS suffix of this computer text box, change the DNS suffix to **cadatum.com** and then click **OK**.

30. Click **OK** to close the Computer Name/Domain Changes text box.

31. When you are prompted to reboot, click **OK**.

32. In the System Properties dialog box, click **Close**.

33. When you are you are prompted to restart the computer, click **Restart Now**.

Exercise 15.2	Creating a Trust Relationship
Overview	In this exercise, you will create a trust relationship between contoso.com and adatum.com and then test the trust relationship.
Mindset	Trusts are relationships between domains or forests that enable a user to be authenticated by domain controllers from another domain. Through trusts, users can access and share resources across security boundaries.
Completion time	60 minutes

1. On CRWDC01, log in using the **contoso\administrator** account and the **Pa$$w0rd** password.

2. In Server Manager, click **Tools > DNS**.

3. In the DNS Manager console, expand **CRWDC01**, click **Conditional Forwarders**, then right-click **Conditional Forwarders** and choose **New Conditional Forwarder**.

4. In the New Conditional Forwarder dialog box, in the DNS Domain text box, type **CAdatum.com**.

5. Click inside the **Click here to add** text box, type in **192.168.1.150** and then press **Enter**. Ignore the red x. Click **OK**.

6. Close **DNS Manager**.

7. On **ARWDC01**, using Server Manager, click **Tools > DNS**.

8. In the DNS Manager console, expand **ARWDC01**.

9. Click **Conditional Forwarders**, right-click **Conditional Forwarders** and choose **New Conditional Forwarder**.

10. In the New Conditional Forwarder dialog box, in the DNS Domain text box, click **contoso.com**.

11. Click inside the **Click here to add** text box, type **192.168.1.50** and then press **Enter**. Disregard the red x and then click **OK**.

12. Under Conditional Forwarders, click **contoso.com**.

13. On the Review Options page, take a screen shot of the DNS Manager window by pressing **Alt+Prt Scr** and then paste it into your Lab 15 worksheet file in the page provided by pressing **Ctrl+V**.

14. Close **DNS Manager**.

15. On **CRWDC01**, using Server Manager, click **Tools > Active Directory Domains and Trusts**.

16. Using Active Directory Domains and Trusts, right-click **contoso.com** and choose **Properties**.

17. In the Properties dialog box, click the **Trusts** tab.

18. Click the **New Trust** button.

19. On the New Trust Wizard page, click **Next**.

20. On the Trust Name page, in the Name text box, type **cadatum** and then click **Next**.

21. On the Trust Type page, click **Forest trust** and then click **Next**.

22. On the Direction of Trust page, select the direction **Two-way** and then click **Next**.

23. On the Sides of Trust page, click **Both this domain and the specified domain** option and then click **Next**.

24. On the User Name and Password page, type the following and then click **Next**:

    User name: **cadatum\administrator**

    Password: **Pa$$w0rd**

25. On the Outgoing Trust Authentication Level-Local Forest page, click **Forest-wide authentication** and then click **Next**.

26. On the Outgoing Trust Authentication Level-Specified Forest page, click **Forest Wide authentication** and then click **Next**.

27. The Trust Selections Complete prompt displays. Click **Next**.

28. On the Confirm Outgoing Trust page, to confirm the trust, select **Yes, confirm the outgoing trust** and then click **Next**.

29. On the Confirm Incoming Trust, to confirm the trust, click **Next**.

30. When the wizard is complete, click **Finish**.

31. Take a screen shot of the contoso.com Properties dialog box by pressing **Alt+Prt Scr** and then paste it into your Lab 15 worksheet file in the page provided by pressing **Ctrl+V**.

32. Click **OK** to close the Properties dialog box.

33. On **CRWDC01**, on the Active Directory Domains and Trusts console, right-click **CONTOSO.COM** and choose **Properties**.

34. In the Properties dialog box, click the **Trusts** tab.

35. Under Domains trusted by this domain (outgoing trusts), click **cadatum.com** and then click **Properties**.

36. In the adatum.com Properties dialog box, click **Validate**.

37. In the Active Directory Domain Services dialog box, click **Yes, validate the incoming trust**.

38. Specify the following and then click **OK**:

Username: **cadatum\administrator**

Password: **Pa$$w0rd**

39. When the trust has been validated and is in place and active, take a screen shot of the Active Directory Domain Services validation message by pressing **Alt+Prt Scr** and then paste it into your Lab 15 worksheet file in the page provided by pressing **Ctrl+V**.

40. Click **OK** to close the Active Directory Domain Services dialog box.

41. In the Active Directory Domain Services dialog box, when you are prompted to update the name suffix routing for this trust, click **No**.

42. Click **OK** to close the adatum.com Properties dialog box.

43. Click **OK** to close the contoso.com Properties dialog box.

44. Close **Active Directory Domains and Trusts**.

45. On **CRWDC01**, open File Explorer by clicking the **File Explorer** icon on the taskbar.

46. Under Computer, click **Local Disk (C:)**. Right-click the white space of the Local Disk (C:) window and choose **New > Folder**. Type **Data** and then press **Enter**.

47. Double-click the **Data** folder.

48. Right-click the white space of the Data folder and choose **New > Text Document**. Name the file **test** and then press **Enter**

49. Click **Local Disk (C:)**. Right-click the **Data** folder and choose **Properties**.

50. In the Properties dialog box, click the **Sharing** tab.

51. Click the **Advanced Sharing** button.

52. In the Advanced Sharing dialog box, click to select **Share this folder**.

53. Click the **Permissions** button.

54. In the Permissions dialog box, grant **Allow Full Control** to Everyone.

55. Click **OK** to close the Permissions dialog box.

56. Click **OK** to close the Advanced Sharing dialog box.

57. In the Data Properties dialog box, click the **Security** tab.

Question 2	Which users can access the Data Properties?

58. Click the **Edit** button.

59. In the Permissions dialog box, click **Add**.

60. In the Select Users, Computers, Service Accounts, or Groups dialog box, click the **Locations** button.

61. In the Locations dialog box, click **cadatum.com** and then click **OK**.

62. In the Enter the object names to select text box, type **domain users**.

63. Click **OK** to close the Permissions dialog box.

64. In the Enter the object names to select text box, type **domain users**.

65. After the Adatum\Domain Users have been added to the ACL, take a screen shot of the Permissions for Data dialog box by pressing **Alt+Prt Scr** and then paste it into your Lab 15 worksheet file in the page provided by pressing **Ctrl+V**.

66. Click to **OK** to close the Permissions for Data dialog box.

67. Click **Close** to close the Data Properties dialog box.

68. On **ARWDC01**, open File Explorer by clicking the **File Explorer** button on the taskbar.

69. Type **\\crwdc01\data** and then press **Enter** key. You should see the test.txt file.

70. Close **File Explorer**.

Exercise 15.3	Installing the Active Directory Migration Tool
Overview	In this exercise, you will first install the .NET Framework and SQL Server. Then you will install the Active Directory Migration Tool.
Mindset	Migrating a domain can be thought of in two different ways. In one situation, you can install a second set of domain controllers and then remove the old domain controllers. In another situation, you must move objects from one domain to another. To perform the following exercise, you will have to use special tools from Microsoft, such as ADMT.
Completion time	70 minutes

1. On **AServer01**, log in using the **contoso\administrator** account and the **Pa$$w0rd** password.

2. Click the **Start** menu, then right-click **Computer** and choose **Properties**.

3. In the System window, click **Change Settings**.

4. In the System Properties dialog box, click **Change**.

5. In the Computer Name/Domain Changes dialog box, click **Domain**. In the Domain text box, type **cadatum** and then click **OK**.

6. In the Windows Security dialog box, login as **administrator** with the password of **Pa$$w0rd**.

7. When a Welcome message appears, click **OK**.

8. Click **OK** to close the Computer Name/Domain Changes dialog box.

9. When a message indicates you must restart your computer, click **OK**.

10. In the System Properties dialog box, click **Close** and then click **Restart Now**.

11. On **AServer01**, log in using the **cadatum\administrator** account and the **Pa$$w0rd** password.

12. Using Server Manager, click **Features > Add Features.**

13. In the **Add Roles and Features** Wizard, click **Next**.

14. In the Add Features Wizard, on the Features page, select **.NET Framework 3.5.1 Features.** When you are prompted to add role services, click **Add Required Role Services**. Click **Next**.

15. On the Select destination server page, click **Next**.

16. On the Select server roles page, click **Next**.

17. On the Select features page, select **.NET Framework 3.5 Features** and then click **Next**.

18. On the Web Server (IIS) page, click **Next**.

19. On the Role Services page, click **Next**.

20. On the Confirmation page, click **Install**.

21. When the installation is complete, click **Close**.

22. Open **File Explorer** by clicking **File Explorer** on the taskbar.

23. Using File Explorer, open the **\\arwdc01\software\SQL2012** folder and

24. On the SQL Server Installation Center page, click **Installation**. Then click **New SQL Server stand-alone installation or add features to an existing installation**. If you are prompted to confirm that you want to run this file, click **Run**.

25. On the Setup Support Rules page, click **OK**.

26. On the Product Key page, select **Specify a free edition** and then click **Next**.

27. On the License Terms page, select **I accept the license terms** and then click **Next**.

28. On the Products Updates page, deselect **Include SQL Server product updates** and then click **Next**.

29. On the Setup Support Rules page, click **Next**.

30. On the Setup Role page, click **Next**.

31. On the Features Selection page, deselect **Database Engine Services** and **Management Tools - Complete**. Click **Next**.

32. On the Installation Rules page, click **Next**.

33. On the Instance Configuration page, click **Next**.

34. On the Disk Space Requirements page, click **Next**.

35. On the Server Configuration page, change the account for SQL Server Database Engine from NT Service\MSSQLSERVER to **cadatum\administrator**. In the corresponding text box, type **Pa$$W0rd** and then click **Next**.

36. On the Database Engine Configuration page, Windows authentication mode is already selected. Click **Add Current User** and then click **Next**.

37. On the Error Reporting page, click **Next**.

38. On the Installation Configuration Rules page, click **Next**.

39. On the Ready to Install page, click **Install**.

40. After several minutes, a message displays, indicating that a computer restart is required. Click **OK**.

41. On the Complete screen, click **Close**.

42. Reboot **AServer01**.

43. On AServer01, log in as **administrator** with the password of **Pa$$w0rd**.

Question 3	*What type of system are you supposed to install the Active Directory Migration Tool to if you want to migrate objects between domain controllers running Windows Server 2012 R2?*

44. On Aserver01, open the **\\crwdc01\software** folder. Then double-click the **admtsetup32.exe**. If a security warning appears, click **Run**.

45. In the Welcome to the Active Directory Migration Tool Installation Wizard, on the Welcome page, click **Next**.

46. On the License Agreement page, select **I Agree**. Click **Next**.

47. On the Customer Experience Improvement Program page, click **Next**.

48. On the Database Selection page, in the Database (Server\Instance) text box, type the name of server and instance and then click **Next**.

49. On the Database Import page, click **Next**.

50. On **AServer01**, log in using the **cadatum\administrator** account and the **Pa$$w0rd** password.

51. Using File Explorer, open the **\\arwdc01\software** folder and double-click **admtsetup32.exe**. If you are prompted to confirm that you want to run this file, click **Run**.

52. In the Welcome to the Active Directory Migration Tool Installation Wizard, on the Welcome page, click **Next**.

53. On the License Agreement page, select **I Agree**. Click **Next**.

54. On the Customer Experience Improvement Program page, click **Next**.

55. On the Database Selection page, in the Database (Server\Instance) text box, type **aserver01** and then click **Next**.

56. When the Active Directory Migration Tool been successfully installed, click **Finish**.

57. When the installation is complete, take a screen shot by pressing **Alt+Prt Scr** and then paste it into your Lab 15 worksheet file in the page provided by pressing **Ctrl+V**.

Exercise 15.4	Migrating a User
Overview	In this exercise, you will create a user and then migrate that user from one forest/domain to another.
Mindset	Users are just one of the objects that will need to be migrated between forests/domains. Other objects include service accounts and global groups. You will also have to Add SIDs to Access Control Lists.
Completion time	30 minutes

1. Log in to CRWDC01 as **cadatum\administrator** with the password of **Pa$$w0rd**.

Question 4	*After you install ADMT, what two things do you need to do if you want to migrate users and groups from one forest/domain to another forest/domain?*

2. Open **Active Directory Users and Computers**.

3. Click the **Builtin** node and then double-click **Administrators**.

4. In the Administrators Properties dialog box, click the **Members** tab and then click the **Add** button.

5. In the Select Users, Contacts, Computers, Service Accounts, and Groups dialog box, click the **Locations** button.

6. In the Location dialog box, select **cadatum.com** and then click **OK**.

7. In the Enter the object names to select text box, type **domain admins** and then click **OK**.

8. Click **OK** to close the Administrators Properties dialog box.

9. Log in to ARWDC01 as **cadatum\administrator** with the password of **Pa$$w0rd**.

10. On ARWDC01, open **Active Directory Users and Computers**. Then create a user with the following characteristics in the Users OU:

First Name: **Jake**

Last Name: **Teason**

User logon name: **JTeason**

Password: **Pa$$w0rd**

11. Close **Active Directory Users and Computers**.

12. On CServer01, click the **Start** button and click **All Programs > Administrative Tools > Active Directory Migration Tool**.

13. In the Active Directory Migration Tool, click **Action > User Account Migration Wizard**.

14. In the User Account Migration Wizard, on the Welcome page, click **Next**.

15. In the Source section, in the Domain text box, type **cadatum.com**. In the Target section, in the Domain text box, type **contoso.com**. Click **Next**.

16. On the User Selection Option page, Select users from domain is already selected. Click **Next**.

17. On the User Selection page, click **Add**.

18. In the Select Users dialog box, in the Enter the object names to select text box, type **Jake Teason** and then click **OK**.

19. Back on the User Selection page, click **Next**.

20. On the Organizational Unit Selection page, in the Target OU, click **Browse**.

21. In the Browse for Container dialog box, select the **Users** OU and then click **OK**.

22. Back on the Organizational Unit Select page, click **Next**.

23. On the Password Options page, answer the next question. Then select the **Generate complex passwords** option and click **Next**.

Question 5	*Where is the password file going to be stored?*

24. On the Account Transition Options page, Click **Next**.

25. On the User Options page, click **Next**.

26. On the Object Property Exclusion page, click **Next**.

27. On the Conflict Management page, click **Next**.

28. On the Completing the user Account Migration Wizard page, click **Finish**.

29. When the migration has been completed, click **Close**.

30. When the object is migrated, take a screen shot of the Migration Progress dialog box by pressing **Alt+Prt Scr** and then paste it into your Lab 15 worksheet file in the page provided by pressing **Ctrl+V**.

End of exercise. Close all windows.

Lab Challenge	Planning a Forest and Domain Infrastructure (Contoso Forest and Domain Infrastructure Project)
Overview	In this written exercise, you will read the background information for the Contoso Corporation provided in Appendix A, then read the information below, and then write your plan. This project is a continuation of Lab 14.
Mindset	You are a new administrator for the Contoso Corporation, which is a leading company in producing smart devices for the home. As a team lead for the Windows Server team, you need to develop a plan to update the Contoso Forest and Domain Infrastructure to Windows Server 2012 R2. In addition, you need assess the best way to reorganize the forest and domain structure. Therefore, you need to determine what needs to be reorganized and how you would reorganize the forest and domain.
Completion time	30 minutes

Create a proposal that includes the following sections:

● Purpose of the Project

● Requirements of the Project

● The Proposed Solution

When writing the proposal, you must explain the reasoning behind your choices.

End of lab.

LAB 16
DESIGNING A GROUP POLICY STRATEGY

BEFORE YOU BEGIN

The lab environment consists of student workstations connected to a local area network, along with a server that functions as the domain controller for a domain called contoso.com. The computers required for this lab are listed in Table 16-1.

Table 16-1
Computers required for Lab 16

Computer	Operating System	Computer Name
Server	Windows Server 2012 R2	CRWDC01
Server	Windows Server 2012 R2	ARWDC01

In addition to the computers, you will also need the software listed in Table 16-2 to complete Lab 16.

Table 16-2
Software required for Lab 16

Software	Location
Lab 16 student worksheet	Lab16_worksheet.docx (provided by instructor)

Working with Lab Worksheets

Each lab in this manual requires that you answer questions, shoot screen shots, and perform other activities that you will document in a worksheet named for the lab, such as Lab16_worksheet.docx. You will find these worksheets on the book companion site. It is recommended that you use a USB flash drive to store your worksheets, so you can submit them to your instructor for review. As you perform the exercises in each lab, open the appropriate worksheet file, fill in the required information, and then save the file to your flash drive.

SCENARIO

After completing this lab, you will be able to:

- Plan and design Group Policy

- Configure loopback processing

- Configure WMI filtering

- Configure slow-link detection for GPOs

- Modify Group Policy caching default settings

- Deploy a site-link GPO

Estimated lab time: 140 minutes

Exercise 16.1	Planning and Designing Group Policy
Overview	In this written exercise, you will read the background information for the Contoso Corporation provided in Appendix A, then read the information below, and then answer the questions.
Mindset	Group Policy is a technology used to configure user and computer settings from a centralized location (Active Directory Domain Services). Domain-joined computers and users can be controlled by administrators, forcing the computers and clients to meet specific policies.
Completion time	20 minutes

Question 1	Which type of policy is processed first?

Question 2	Typically, which policy is not added to GPO settings?

Question 3	What should you do to ensure certain GPO settings are not overwritten by other policies?

Question 4	A company application includes a 32-bit version and a 64-bit version. How can you ensure that 32-bit machines get the 32-bit version and 64-bit machines get the 64-bit version?

Question 5	You want to create several kiosk machines for the lobby. However, you want to ensure certain settings are applied to the kiosk computer no matter who logs on. What can you do?

Question 6	You administer an OU that is used for testing. How can you block most of the GPOs?

Exercise 16.2	Configuring Loopback Processing
Overview	In this exercise, the computer settings will overwrite user settings when applying GPO settings for a GPO (GPO1) that you will create. Unlike the approach used in previous courses, you will not be guided through each step. Instead, you must determine the best way to perform the task based on the guidelines provided.
Mindset:	You are responsible for establishing a multiple-kiosk computer that will be used in the front lobby of your company. You want to ensure that the configuration of the computer is the same regardless of who logs on. How can you do it?
Completion time	10 minutes

Take a screen shot of the Configure User Group Policy Loopback Processing Mode dialog box that shows the settings by pressing **Alt+Prt Scr** and then paste it into your Lab 16 worksheet file in the page provided by pressing **Ctrl+V**.

Exercise 16.3	Configuring WMI Filtering
Overview	In this exercise, you will fine-tune the processing of GPOs by using WMI filtering that will affect only 32-bit machines. Unlike the approach used in previous courses, you will not be guided through each step. Instead, you must determine the best way to perform the task based on the guidelines provided.
Mindset	Using the WMI Query Language, administrators can filter based on several hardware and software criteria. When added to Group Policy Objects, WMI Filters will filter the targeted systems and filter based on the specified criteria.
Completion time	15 minutes

Take a screen shot of the Configure user Group Policy Loopback Processing Mode dialog box that shows the settings by pressing **Alt+Prt Scr** and then paste it into your Lab 16 worksheet file in the page provided by pressing **Ctrl+V**.

Exercise 16.4	Configuring Slow-Link Detection
Overview	In this exercise, you will configure a Group Policy to define a slow links as 1000 KBps. Unlike the approach used in previous courses, you will not be guided through each step. Instead, you must determine the best way to perform the task based on the guidelines provided.
Mindset	Defined in kilobytes per second (KBps), links between a client and the nearest domain controller are measured. A link slower than 500 KBps is considered a slow link.
Completion time	10 minutes

Take a screen shot of the Configure Group Policy Slow Link Detection dialog box that shows the settings by pressing **Alt+Prt Scr** and then paste it into your Lab 16 worksheet file in the page provided by pressing **Ctrl+V**.

Exercise 16.5	Modifying the Group Policy Caching Defaults
Overview	In this exercise, you will enable Group Policy Caching. Unlike the approach used in previous courses, you will not be guided through each step. Instead, you must determine the best way to enable Group Policy Caching based on the guidelines provided.
Mindset	Turned on by default in Windows Server 2012 R2 and Windows 8.1, Group Policy Caching pulls certain GPOs from the domain controller and stores them locally on the client computer for faster load times at the next network logon.
Completion time	5 minutes

Take a screen shot of the Configure Group Policy Caching dialog box that shows the settings by pressing **Alt+Prt Scr** and then paste it into your Lab 16 worksheet file in the page provided by pressing **Ctrl+V**.

Exercise 16.6	Deploying a Site-Link GPO
Overview	In this exercise, you will link the GPO to Site2.
Mindset	Group Policy Objects linked at the site level apply first to all users and computers located within that site. Site-linked GPOs will, in turn, affect all users and computers of all domains within the forest located in that site. This means that if three domains have objects located within one site, a GPO linked to the site will apply to every user and computer in that site.
Completion time	10 minutes

1. On CRWDC01, using Server Manager, open **Active Directory Sites and Services**.

Question 7	Which GPO executes first: domain level, organizational units, or sites?

2. Right-click **Sites** and choose **New Site**.

3. In the New Object – Site dialog box, in the Name text box, type **Site2**. Select **DEFAULTIPSITELINK** and then click **OK**.

4. When the site has been created, click **OK**.

5. Close the **Active Directory Sites and Services**.

6. Using Group Policy Management Console, right-click the **Sites** node and choose **Show Sites**.

7. In the Show Sites dialog box, click **Select All** and then click **OK**.

8. Right-click **Site2** and choose **Link an Existing GPO**.

9. In the Select GPO dialog box, click **GPO1** and then click **OK**.

10. Click the **Site2** node.

11. Take a screen shot of the Group Policy Management console by pressing **Alt+Prt Scr** and then paste it into your Lab 16 worksheet file in the page provided by pressing **Ctrl+V**.

Lab Challenge	Planning a Group Policy (Contoso Group Policy Project)
Overview	In this written exercise, you will read the background information for the Contoso Corporation provided in Appendix A, then read the information below, and then write your plan.
Mindset	You are a new administrator for the Contoso Corporation, which is a leading company in producing smart devices for the home. Your manager wants you to review the GPOs and determine the best strategy to deploy when using and managing GPOs. He also wants you to recommend GPO settings that should be applied.
Completion time	70 minutes

Create a proposal that includes the following sections:

- Purpose of the Project
- Requirements of the Project
- The Proposed Solution

When writing the proposal, you must explain the reasoning behind your choices.

End of lab.

LAB 17
DESIGNING AN ACTIVE DIRECTORY PERMISSION MODEL

THIS LAB CONTAINS THE FOLLOWING EXERCISES AND ACTIVITIES:

Exercise 17.1   Planning an Active Directory Permission Model

Exercise 17.2   Customizing Tasks Using the Delegation of Control Wizard

Exercise 17.3   Delegating Permissions to AdminSDHolder

Exercise 17.4   Configuring Kerberos and Kerberos Delegation

Lab Challenge   Planning and Designing an Active Directory Permission Model
                     (Contoso Active Directory Permission Model Project)

BEFORE YOU BEGIN

The lab environment consists of student workstations connected to a local area network, along with a server that functions as the domain controller for a domain called contoso.com. The computers required for this lab are listed in Table 17-1.

Table 17-1
Computers required for Lab 17

Computer	Operating System	Computer Name
Server	Windows Server 2012 R2	CRWDC01

In addition to the computers, you will also need the software listed in Table 17-2 to complete Lab 17.

Table 17-2
Software required for Lab 17

Software	Location
Lab 17 student worksheet	Lab17_worksheet.docx (provided by instructor)

Working with Lab Worksheets

Each lab in this manual requires that you answer questions, shoot screen shots, and perform other activities that you will document in a worksheet named for the lab, such as Lab17_worksheet.docx. You will find these worksheets on the book companion site. It is recommended that you use a USB flash drive to store your worksheets, so you can submit them to your instructor for review. As you perform the exercises in each lab, open the appropriate worksheet file, fill in the required information, and then save the file to your flash drive.

SCENARIO

After completing this lab, you will be able to:

- Plan and design an Active Directory Permission Model

- Customize tasks using the Delegation of Control Wizard

- Delegate permissions to AdminSDHolder

- Configure Kerberos and Kerberos Delegation

- Plan and design an Active Directory Permission Model

Estimated lab time: 115 minutes

Exercise 17.1	Planning an Active Directory Permission Model
Overview	In this written exercise, you will read the background information for the Contoso Corporation provided in Appendix A, then read the information below, and then write your plan.
Mindset	Active Directory consists of objects. Similar to NTFS permissions, Active Directory has permissions that specify what users can do with specified Active Directory objects.
Completion time	10 minutes

Question 1	*Is it rights or is it permissions that specify who can manage users and groups?*

Question 2	*You administer an organizational unit that contains all printers. What is the easiest way to assign a user so that the user can manage printers?*

Question 3	*How should you manage Active Directory users and computers from your Windows 8.1 machine?*

Question 4	*Which level should you assign a GPO that will configure Kerberos settings?*

Exercise 17.2	Customizing Tasks to Delegate of Control Wizard
Overview	In this exercise, you will create an OU and then delegate control of the OU.
Mindset	The Delegation of Control Wizard provides the easiest and most efficient way to assign permissions to an organizational unit so that the user or group can manage the organizational unit or perform some administrative function. By using the Delegation of Control Wizard, you can assign the minimum permission that the user or users need in order to complete their authorized tasks.
Completion time	15 minutes

1. Log in to CRWDC01 as **contoso\administrator** with the password of **Pa$$w0rd**.

2. On the CRWDC01, using Server Manager, open **Active Directory Users and Computers** console.

3. Right-click **contoso.com** and choose **New**. Then create the **Printer OU**.

4. Right-click the **Printer** OU and choose **New**. Then create a Global Security group named **PrinterAdmins**.

5. Right-click the **Printers** OU and choose **Delegate Control**.

6. In the Delegation of Control Wizard, on the Welcome screen, click **Next**.

7. On the Users or Groups page, click **Add**.

8. In the Select Users, Computers, or Groups dialog box, in the Enter the object names to select box, type **printadmin** and then click **OK**.

9. Back on the Users or Groups page, click **Next**.

10. On the Tasks to Delegate page, select the following:

    - Create, delete, and manage user accounts.
    - Create, delete, and manage groups
    - Modify the membership of a group

    Click **Next**.

Question 5	What you would do if you only want the specified users to only manage computers?

11. When the wizard is complete, click **Finish**.

12. Right-click the **Printers** OU and choose **Properties**. Click the **Security** tab.

13. Click the **Advanced** button.

14. When the Advanced Security Settings for Printers opens, take a screen shot by pressing **Alt+Prt Scr** and then paste it into your Lab 17 worksheet file in the page provided by pressing **Ctrl+V**.

15. Click **OK** to close the Advanced Security Settings for Printers dialog box.

16. Click **OK** to close the Printers Properties dialog box.

Exercise 17.3	Delegating Permissions to AdminSDHolder
Overview	In this exercise, you will delegate permissions to AdminSDHolder using Active Directory users and Computers.
Mindset	The AdminSDHolder is used to secure privileged users and groups from unintentional modification. Every hour, the security permissions of the privileged group will be compared to the permissions listed in the AdminSDHolder object and reset them if they are different.
Completion time	15 minutes

1. On CRWDC01, log in using the **contoso\administrator** account and the **Pa$$w0rd** password.

2. Using Server Manager or Administrative Tools, open **Active Directory Users and Computers**. If needed, expand the **Contoso.com** node.

3. In the Users folder, in the **Users** OU, create an account named **SPAdmin**.

4. If you cannot see the System node, click **View > Advanced Features**.

5. Expand the **System** node.

6. Right-click **AdminSDHolder** and choose **Properties**.

7. In the **AdminSDHolder** Properties dialog box, click the **Security** tab.

8. Click the **Advanced** button.

Question 6	*What are some of the groups that are protected with AdminSDHolder?*

9. Click the **Enable Inheritance** button and then click **Apply**. If you are prompted to continue, click **Yes**.

10. Click **Add**.

11. In the Permission Entry for AdminSDHolder dialog box, click the **Select a principal** link.

12. In the Select User, Computer, Service Account, or Group dialog box, in the Enter the object name to select, type **SPAdmin** and then click **OK**.

13. Under Permissions, select **Full Control** and then click **OK**.

14. Click **OK** to close the Advanced Security Settings for AdminSDHolder dialog box.

15. Take a screen shot of the AdminSDHolder Properties dialog box by pressing **Alt+Prt Scr** and then paste it into your Lab 17 worksheet file in the page provided by pressing **Ctrl+V**.

16. Click **OK** to close the AdminSDHolder Properties dialog box.

Exercise 17.4	Configuring Kerberos and Kerberos Delegation
Overview	In this exercise, you will create a Service Principal Name (SPN) for an account and then configure Kerberos delegation.
Mindset	An SPN is the name by which a client uniquely identifies an instance of a service. The client locates the service based on the SPN, which consists of three components: The service class, such as HTTP (which includes both the HTTP and HTTPS protocols) or SQLService; the host name; and the port (if port 80 is not being used).
Completion time	15 minutes

1. On CRWDC01, using Server Manager, click **Tools > ADSI Edit**. The ADSI Edit console opens.

2. Right-click **ADSI Edit** in the console tree and choose **Connect To**. In the Connection Settings dialog box, click **OK**.

3. Double-click Default Naming Context in the console tree, expand **DC=contoso,DC=com**, and then click **OU=Users**.

4. In the Details pane, right-click **CN=SPAdmin** and choose **Properties**. The CN=SPAdmin Properties dialog box opens.

5. In the Attributes list, double-click **servicePrincipalName** to display the Multi-valued String Editor dialog box.

6. In the Value to add field, type **http/portal.contoso.com:443** and then click **Add**.

7. Click **OK** twice.

8. Using Server Manager, click **Tools > Active Directory Users and Computers**.

9. Navigate to and click the **Users** organizational unit.

10. Right-click **SPAdmin** and choose **Properties**. The Properties dialog box opens.

11. Click the **Delegation** tab.

12. To allow this account to be delegated for a service, click **Trust this user for delegation to any service (Kerberos only)**.

13. Take a screen shot of the SPAdmin Properties Delegation tab by pressing **Alt+Prt Scr** and then paste it into your Lab 17 worksheet file in the page provided by pressing **Ctrl+V**.

Question 7	How would you specify how long Kerberos tickets last?

14. Click **OK**.

Lab Challenge	Planning and Designing an Active Directory Permission Model (Contoso Active Directory Permission Model Project)
Overview	In this written exercise, you will read the background information for the Contoso Corporation provided in Appendix A, then read the information below, and then write your plan.
Mindset	You are a new administrator for the Contoso Corporation, which is a leading company in producing smart devices for the home. You schedule a meeting with your manager to discuss tightening up Active Directory security. You are to develop a plan that outlines the company's Active Directory security policy.
Completion time	60 minutes

Create a proposal that includes the following sections:

● Purpose of the Project

● Requirements of the Project

● The Proposed Solution

When writing the proposal, you must explain the reasoning behind your choices.

End of lab.

LAB 18
DESIGNING AN ACTIVE DIRECTORY SITES TOPOLOGY

THIS LAB CONTAINS THE FOLLOWING EXERCISES AND ACTIVITIES:

Exercise 18.1   Designing an Active Directory Sites Topology

Exercise 18.2   Adding Sites and Subnets

Exercise 18.3   Promoting a CServer01 to a Domain Controller

Exercise 18.4   Monitoring Active Directory Replication Using the Active Directory Replication Status Tool

Lab Challenge   Planning and Designing an Active Directory Sites Topology and Domain Controller Strategy (Contoso Active Directory Sites Topology and Domain Controller Project)

BEFORE YOU BEGIN

The lab environment consists of student workstations connected to a local area network, along with a server that functions as the domain controller for a domain called contoso.com. The computers required for this lab are listed in Table 18-1.

Table 18-1
Computers required for Lab 18

Computer	Operating System	Computer Name
Server	Windows Server 2012 R2	CRWDC01
Server	Windows Server 2012 R2	CServer01

In addition to the computers, you will also need the software listed in Table 18-2 to complete Lab 18.

Table 18-2
Software required for Lab 18

Software	Location
Lab 18 student worksheet	Lab18_worksheet.docx (provided by instructor)

Working with Lab Worksheets

Each lab in this manual requires that you answer questions, shoot screen shots, and perform other activities that you will document in a worksheet named for the lab, such as Lab18_worksheet.docx. You will find these worksheets on the book companion site. It is recommended that you use a USB flash drive to store your worksheets, so you can submit them to your instructor for review. As you perform the exercises in each lab, open the appropriate worksheet file, fill in the required information, and then save the file to your flash drive.

SCENARIO

After completing this lab, you will be able to:

- Design an Active Directory Sites Topology

- Add Sites and Services

- Promote a server to a domain controller

- Monitor Active Directory Replication using the Active Directory Replication Status Tool

Estimated lab time: 155 minutes

Exercise 18.1	Design an Active Directory Sites Topology
Overview	In this written exercise, you will read the background information for the Contoso Corporation provided in Appendix A, then read the information below, and then answer the questions.
Mindset	Active Directory domains, trees, and forests provide a logical representation of your network organization, which allows you to organize them in the best way to manage them. To identify domains, trees, and forests, Active Directory is closely tied to DNS. Sites and domain controllers, however, represent the physical structure of your network.
Completion time	20 minutes

Question 1	You just started working at the Contoso Corporation. Before you determine what the Active Directory Sites Topology, what should you do?

Question 2	You determine that not every site needs a domain controller. Why will you need to have a local domain controller?

Question 3	What are the primary reasons for creating multiple AD DS sites?

Question 4	What is the minimum bandwidth for a site link to be considered well connected?

Question 5	When you create a site, how is the site defined so that it knows which hosts are part of a site?

Question 6	Which type of replication should be used for the Contoso Corporation:, Intersite replication or intrasite replication?

Question 7	Which replication model should be used for the Contoso Corporation? Why?

Question 8	Which links would have the lowest site costs for the Contoso Corporation?

Question 9	How many domain controllers should be placed at the Miami site? Why?

Question 10	How many domain controllers should be place in a sales office?

Exercise 18.2	Adding Sites and Subnets
Overview	In this exercise, you will create a site for Detroit, which will use the 192.168.5.0/24 subnet, and you will create a site for Miami, which will use 192.168.10.0/24. Unlike the approach used in previous courses, you will not be guided through each step. Instead, you must determine the best way to complete the tasks required based on the guidelines provided.
Mindset	Active Directory uses sites and subnets to determine how to replicate data between domain controllers. Sites allow clients, authentication, and applications to access domain controllers within a physical location instead of going across a slower WAN link.
Completion time	15 minutes

After the sites and subnets have been created, take a screen shot of Active Directory Sites and Services of the Subnets node by pressing **Alt+Prt Scr** and then paste it into your Lab 18 worksheet file in the page provided by pressing **Ctrl+V**.

Exercise 18.3	Promoting a CServer01 to a Domain Controller
Overview	In this exercise, you will install the Active Directory Domain services and then promote a server to a domain controller. Unlike the approach used in previous courses, you will not be guided through each step. Instead, you must determine the best way to complete the required tasks based on the guidelines provided.
Mindset	Unlike the approach used in previous courses, you will not be guided through each step. Instead, you must determine the best way to deploy the application based on the guidelines provided.
Completion time	30 minutes

After the installation is finished, open the Active Directory Users and Computers, take a screen shot of Active Directory Sites and Services of the Domain Controllers node by pressing **Alt+Prt** Scr and then paste it into your Lab18 worksheet file in the page provided by pressing **Ctrl+V**.

Exercise 18.4	Monitoring Active Directory Replication Using the Active Directory Replication Status Tool
Overview	In this exercise, you will install the Active Directory Replication Status Tool. Then you will use the tool to check the Active Directory replication status between two domain controllers. Unlike the approach used in previous courses, you will not be guided through each step. Instead, you must determine the best way to complete the required tasks based on the guidelines provided.
Mindset	Released by Microsoft in 2012, the Active Directory Replication Status Tool (ADREPLSTATUS) allows for much simpler and straightforward monitoring and troubleshooting, taking the results returned and placing them into an easy-to-use application.
Completion time	30 minutes

Take a screen shot of AD Replication Status Tool showing the Replication Status Viewer tab by pressing **Alt+Prt Scr** and then paste it into your Lab 18 worksheet file in the page provided by pressing **Ctrl+V**.

Lab Challenge	Planning and Designing an Active Directory Sites Topology and Domain Controller Strategy (Contoso Active Directory Sites Topology and Domain Controller Project)
Overview	In this written exercise, you will read the background information for the Contoso Corporation provided in Appendix A, then read the information below, and then write your plan. This exercise will continue in Lab 19 and Lab 20.
Mindset	You are a new administrator for the Contoso Corporation, which is a leading company in producing smart devices for the home. You need to optimize the Active Directory Sites Topology. Therefore, you will need to develop a plan on how to define the sites, subnets, link costs, domain controllers, global catalogs and operations masters for the company.
Completion time	60 minutes

Create a proposal that includes the following sections:

- Purpose of the Project
- Requirements of the Project
- The Proposed Solution

When writing the proposal, you must explain the reasoning behind your choices.

End of lab.

LAB 19
DESIGNING A DOMAIN CONTROLLER STRATEGY

THIS LAB CONTAINS THE FOLLOWING EXERCISES AND ACTIVITIES:

Exercise 19.1   Designing a Domain Controller Strategy

Exercise 19.2   Adding Attributes to the Partial Attributes Set

Exercise 19.3   Transferring the Operations Masters Role

Exercise 19.4   Installing a Read-Only Domain Controller (RODC)

Lab Challenge   Planning and Designing an Active Directory Sites Topology and Domain Controller Strategy (Contoso Active Directory Sites Topology and Domain Controller Project)

BEFORE YOU BEGIN

The lab environment consists of student workstations connected to a local area network, along with a server that functions as the domain controller for a domain called contoso.com. The computers required for this lab are listed in Table 19-1.

Table 19-1
Computers required for Lab 19

Computer	Operating System	Computer Name
Server	Windows Server 2012 R2	CRWDC01
Server	Windows Server 2012 R2	CServer01
Server	Windows Server 2012 R2	CServer02

In addition to the computers, you will also need the software listed in Table 19-2 to complete Lab 19.

Table 19-2
Software required for Lab 19

Software	Location
Lab 19 student worksheet	Lab19_worksheet.docx (provided by instructor)

Working with Lab Worksheets

Each lab in this manual requires that you answer questions, shoot screen shots, and perform other activities that you will document in a worksheet named for the lab, such as Lab19_worksheet.docx. You will find these worksheets on the book companion site. It is recommended that you use a USB flash drive to store your worksheets, so you can submit them to your instructor for review. As you perform the exercises in each lab, open the appropriate worksheet file, fill in the required information, and then save the file to your flash drive.

SCENARIO

After completing this lab, you will be able to:

- Design and plan a domain controller strategy

- Add attributes to the partial attributes set

- Transfer the Operations Master role

- Install an RODC

Estimated lab time: 125 minutes

Exercise 19.1	Designing a Domain Controller Strategy
Overview	In this written exercise, you will read the background information for the Contoso Corporation provided in Appendix A, then read the information below, and then answer the questions.
Mindset	Domain controllers are the servers that store and run the Active Directory database. Active Directory is a major component in authentication, authorization, and auditing. Therefore, you need to understand what the domain controller does, how many domain controllers you need, where to deploy them, and how to configure them.
Completion time	10 minutes

Question 1	At the Contoso Corporation, how many domain controllers should you make global catalogs?

Question 2	For the Contoso Corporation, where should the PDC Emulator be placed? Why?

Question 3	For the Contoso Corporation, what should be changed in the deployment of the Operations Master roles?

Question 4	A sales office does not seem to be secure. You also must accelerate the time it takes for users to authenticate. What can you do?

Exercise 19.2	Adding Attributes to the Partial Attributes Set
Overview	In this exercise, you will add the assistant attribute to the partial attributes set so that it can be replicated to all global catalogs in the forest.
Mindset	As mentioned in the previous section, the global catalog contains a partial copy of all objects from other domains in the forest. The partial copy includes attributes (partial attribute set), which are commonly used in search and other applications. The reason that only a partial copy is replicated to all domain controllers in other domains is to reduce the amount of replication traffic and to minimize the size of the Active Directory database.
Completion time	10 minutes

1. On CRWDC01, log in using the **contoso\administrator** account and the **Pa$$w0rd** password.

2. Right-click the **Start** button and choose **Command Prompt (Admin)**.

Question 5	Which group can make changes to the scheme?

3. At the command prompt window, to register the Active Directory Schema, execute the **regsvr32 schmmgmt.dll** command. When the dll file is registered, click **OK**.

4. At the command prompt, execute the **mmc** command.

5. On the console, click **File > Add/Remove Snap-in**.

6. On the Add or Remove Snap-ins dialog box, click **Active Directory Schema** and then click **Add**.

7. To close the Add or Remove Snap-ins dialog inbox, click **OK**.

8. Expand the Active Directory Schema node and then click the **Attributes** node.

9. In the right pane, scroll down to the **assistant** attribute, right-click the **assistant** attribute, and then choose **Properties**.

10. Click to select the **Replicate this attribute to the Global Catalog** check box.

11. Take a screen shot of the assistant Properties dialog box by pressing **Alt+Prt Scr** and then paste it into your Lab 19 worksheet file in the page provided by pressing **Ctrl+V**.

12. Click **OK**.

Exercise 19.3	Transferring the Operations Masters Role
Overview	In this exercise, transfer the RID master to CServer01. Unlike the approach used in previous courses, you will not be guided through each step. Instead, you must determine the best way to complete the required tasks based on the guidelines provided.
Mindset	From time to time, you might need to move the operation master roles to other domain controllers. If you are planning to do maintenance during which a domain controller that holds the Operations Master will be down for an extended period of time, you are going to retire a domain controller that holds a role of Operations Master, or you need to move the role to a domain controller with more resources, you will need to transfer the Operations Master. Transferring a FSMO role requires that the source domain controller and the target domain controller be online.
Completion time	15 minutes

When the operations master role is successfully transferred, take a screen shot by pressing **Alt+Prt Scr** and then paste it into your Lab 19 worksheet file in the page provided by pressing **Ctrl+V**.

Exercise 19.4	Installing a Read-Only Domain Controller (RODC)
Overview	In this exercise, you will promote CServer02 to a read-only domain controller. Unlike the approach used in previous courses, you will not be guided through each step. Instead, you must determine the best way to complete the required tasks based on the guidelines provided.
Mindset	Windows Server 2012 and Windows Server 2012 R2 include the read-only domain controller (RODC), which contains a full replication of the domain database. It was created to be used in places where a domain controller is needed but the physical security of the domain controller could not be guaranteed.
Completion time	30 minutes

On the Review Options page, when you are promoting the server to the domain controller, take a screen shot by pressing **Alt+Prt Scr** and then paste it into your Lab 19 worksheet file in the page provided by pressing **Ctrl+V**.

Lab Challenge	Planning and Designing an Active Directory Sites Topology and Domain Controller Strategy (Contoso Active Directory Sites Topology and Domain Controller Project)
Overview	In this written exercise, you will read the background information for the Contoso Corporation provided in Appendix A, then read the information below, and then write your plan. This exercise continues from Lab 18 and will continue into Lab 20.
Mindset	You are a new administrator for the Contoso Corporation, which is a leading company in producing smart devices for the home. You need to optimize the Active Directory Sites Topology. Therefore, you will need to develop a plan on how to define the sites, subnets, link costs, domain controllers, global catalogs and operations masters for the company.
Completion time	60 minutes

Create a proposal that includes the following sections:

- Purpose of the Project
- Requirements of the Project
- The Proposed Solution

When writing the proposal, you must explain the reasoning behind your choices.

End of lab.

LAB 20
DESIGNING A FOREST AND DOMAIN INFRASTRUCTURE

BEFORE YOU BEGIN

The lab environment consists of student workstations connected to a local area network, along with a server that functions as the domain controller for a domain called contoso.com. The computers required for this lab are listed in Table 20-1.

Table 20-1
Computers required for Lab 20

Computer	Operating System	Computer Name
Server	Windows Server 2012 R2	CRWDC01
Server	Windows Server 2012 R2	CServer01
Server	Windows Server 2012 R2	CServer03

In addition to the computers, you will also need the software listed in Table 20-2 to complete Lab 20.

Table 20-2
Software required for Lab 20

Software	Location
Lab 20 student worksheet	Lab20_worksheet.docx (provided by instructor)

Working with Lab Worksheets

Each lab in this manual requires that you answer questions, shoot screen shots, and perform other activities that you will document in a worksheet named for the lab, such as Lab20_worksheet.docx. You will find these worksheets on the book companion site. It is recommended that you use a USB flash drive to store your worksheets, so you can submit them to your instructor for review. As you perform the exercises in each lab, open the appropriate worksheet file, fill in the required information, and then save the file to your flash drive.

SCENARIO

After completing this lab, you will be able to:

- Design a branch office infrastructure

- Implement BranchCache

Estimated lab time: 115 minutes

Exercise 20.1	Designing a Branch Office Infrastructure
Overview	In this written exercise, you will read the background information for the Contoso Corporation provided in Appendix A, then read the information below, and then answer the questions.
Mindset	Windows Server 2012, Windows Server 2012 R2, Windows 8, and Windows 8.1 have devoted a great deal of attention to branch office computing and the complications that distance and isolation present to IT administrators. However, before branch office administrators can take charge, enterprise administrators must create the policies that the branch offices will follow.
Completion time	15 minutes

Question 1	How many administrators should you have at the Miami site?

Question 2	How many administrators should you have in the sales office?

Question 3	For the sales office, if you do not have a domain controller, what should you enable?

Question 4	You want to ensure that your special admin accounts are not replicated to your RODCs. What should you do?

Question 5	The sales office does not have a dedicated file server. Several users repeatedly access the same sales documents that are stored at the corporate office. Because they have limited bandwidth, how can you best use the WAN links?

Exercise 20.2	Implementing BranchCache
Overview	In this exercise, you will implement BranchCache so that files accessed from the corporate office will be cached.
Mindset	BranchCache is designed to optimize the link between branch offices and main offices by caching information from content servers on local computers within the branch. This reduces traffic on the WAN links, reduces response time for opening files, and improves the experience for users connecting over slow links.
Completion time	40 minutes

1. Log in to CServer01 as **contoso\administrator** with the password of **Pa$$w0rd**.

2. On CServer01, using Server Manager, click **Manage > Add Roles and Features**. The Add Roles and Feature Wizard opens.

3. In the Add Roles and Features Wizard, click **Next**.

4. On the Select Installation Type page, make sure that **Role-based or feature-based installation** is selected and then click **Next**.

5. On the Select destination server page, click **CServer01.contoso.com** and then click **Next**.

6. In Select Server Roles, under Roles, expand **File and Storage Services** and then expand **File and iSCSI Services**. Click to select the check box for **BranchCache for Network Files** and then click **Next**.

7. In Select features, click **BranchCache** and then click **Next**.

Question 6	What does the BranchCache feature do?

8. On the Confirm installation selections page, click **Install**. When installation is complete, click **Close**.

9. Log in to CRWDC01 as **contoso\administrator** with the password of **Pa$$w0rd**.

10. On CRWDC01, in Server Manager, click **Tools > Active Directory Users and Computers**.

11. In the Active Directory Users and Computers console, right-click **contoso.com** and choose **New > Organizational Unit**.

12. In the New Object – Organization Unit dialog box, in the Name text box, type **Servers**. Click **OK**.

13. Close **Active Directory Users and Computers**.

14. On CRWDC01, in Server Manager, click **Tools > Group Policy Management**. The Group Policy Management console opens.

15. Navigate to and right-click the **Servers** OU and then choose **Create a GPO in this domain, and Link it here**.

16. In the New GPO dialog box, in the Name text box, type **BranchCache for Servers**.

17. Click **OK** to close the New GPO dialog box.

18. Expand the **Servers** OU and right-click the **BranchCache for Servers** GPO and choose **Edit**.

19. In the Group Policy Management Editor, expand the following path: **Computer Configuration, Policies, Administrative Templates, Network**. Under **Network**, click **Lanman Server**.

20. Double-click **Hash Publication for BranchCache**. The Hash Publication for BranchCache dialog box opens.

21. In the Hash Publication for BranchCache dialog box, click **Enabled**.

22. In Options, **Allow hash publication for all shared folders** is already selected. To enable hash publication for all shared folders in all file servers that you add to the OU, click **Allow hash publication for all shared folders**.

23. Click **OK** to close the Hash Publication for BranchCache dialog box.

24. Close **Group Policy Management Editor**.

25. On CServer01, open File Explorer by clicking the **File Explorer** icon on the taskbar.

26. Create a folder named **C:\SharedFolder**.

27. Right-click the **C:\SharedFolder** and choose **Properties**.

28. Click the **Sharing** tab and click **Advanced Sharing**.

29. Click **Share this folder** and then click **OK** to close the Advanced Sharing dialog box.

30. Click **Close** to close the SharedFolder Properties dialog box.

31. Close **File Explorer**.

32. On CServer01, in **Server Manager**, click **Tools > Computer Management**.

33. In the Computer Management console, under **System Tools**, expand **Shared Folders** and then click **Shares**.

34. In the details pane, right-click **SharedFolder** and choose **Properties**. The share's Properties dialog box opens.

35. In the Properties dialog box, on the General tab, click **Offline Settings**. The Offline Settings dialog box opens.

36. Ensure that **Only the files and programs that users specify are available offline** is selected and then click **Enable BranchCache**.

37. Take a screen shot of the Offline Settings dialog box by pressing **Alt+Prt Scr** and then paste it into your Lab 20 worksheet file in the page provided by pressing **Ctrl+V**.

38. Click **OK** twice.

39. Close **Computer Management**.

40. On CRWDC01, using Group Policy Management, expand **Group Policy Objects** and then right-click **Default Domain Policy** and choose **Edit**.

41. In the Group Policy Management Editor, navigate to the **Computer Configuration > Policies > Administrative Templates > Network** node and click **BranchCache**.

42. Double-click **Set BranchCache Distributed Cache mode**.

43. In the **Set BranchCache Distributed Cache mode** dialog box, click **Enabled**.

44. Click **OK** to close the Set BranchCache Distributed Cache mode.

45. Take a screen shot by pressing **Alt+Prt Scr** and then paste it into your Lab 20 worksheet file in the page provided by pressing **Ctrl+V**.

46. Close **Group Policy Management Editor**.

47. Close **Group Policy Management**.

Lab Challenge	Planning and Designing an Active Directory Sites Topology and Domain Controller Strategy (Contoso Active Directory Sites Topology and Domain Controller Project)
Overview	In this written exercise, you will read the background information for the Contoso Corporation provided in Appendix A, then read the information below, and then write your plan. This exercise continues from Lab 19.
Mindset	You are a new administrator for the Contoso Corporation, which is a leading company in producing smart devices for the home. You need to optimize the Active Directory Sites Topology. Therefore, you will need to develop a plan on how to define the sites, subnets, link costs, domain controllers, global catalogs and operations masters for the company.
Completion time	60 minutes

Create a proposal that includes the following sections:

● Purpose of the Project

● Requirements of the Project

● The Proposed Solution

When writing the proposal, you must explain the reasoning behind your choices.

End of lab.

APPENDIX A
CONTOSO CORPORATION OVERVIEW

The Contoso Corporation is a leading company in producing smart devices for the home including smart doors, smart vacuums, smart lamps, smart heating and cooling systems, smart windows, smart shades, smart clocks, smart exercise equipment, smart dishwashers, smart refrigerators, smart televisions, smart radios, smart beds, smart chairs, and smart sinks. The Contoso Corporation began as a security system consultant company consisting of 5 workers, and has grown to an international company with 8,000 employees.

PHYSICAL SITES

The Corporate office is in Sacramento, California with a campus consisting of three buildings.

- Building Sacramento-A: Offices for 400 employees. Sacramento-A hosts a large number of executives including the president, most of the vice-presidents, the chief financial officer, and chief information officer. It also includes corporate marketing team, corporate accounting team, and corporate legal team. The main information technology is located in Building Sacramento-A as well as the largest data center from the company.

- Building Sacramento-B: Offices for 320 employees consisting of the corporate design and testing teams.

- Building Sacramento-C: Offices for 420 employees consisting of the marketing team, corporate sales team, and miscellaneous staff positions.

The Contoso Corporation has grown quickly by purchasing other companies so that they could access patents, designs, and technical staff for various products and technology. As a result, the Contoso Corporation has 8 manufacturing sites containing between 300–500 employees each. Each of the manufacturing sites consists of a server room. The Manufacturing sites include:

- Detroit
- Miami
- Dallas
- Pittsburgh
- Phoenix
- Seattle
- Oklahoma City
- Portland

The call center, which handles customer questions and problems, is located in Cleveland. The call center is open 24/7 with 380 to 560 users depending on the volume and season. There are 4 distribution centers in Reno, Austin, Albany, and Denver. Each site has 300 to 400 employees.

The majority of the other employees are sales personnel and in-house consultants, who create customized solutions for home owners throughout the United States. They reside in 78 sites, each containing between 10 and 25 employees.

Recently, the Contoso Corporation has purchased a company called Adatum Incorporated, which is located in Chicago. Adatum Incorporated employs 130 users. However, since some of the positions will be redundant, you should expect that approximately 30 users will be terminated.

ACTIVE DIRECTORY

The Contoso Corporation uses two forests. The primary forest/domain is contoso.com. There is also a subdomain called support.contoso.com.

In the Contoso.com domain, you have the following organizational units:

- Executives
- Marketing
- Accounting
- Legal
- Design
- Testing
- Information Technology
- Sales
- Distribution

In the support.contoso.com domain, you have the following organizational units:

- Managers
- Call Personnel

The forest/domain for Adatum Incorporated is adatum.com. While Adatum Incorporated has its own IT team, you will be taking over their resources and eventually merge the Adatum resources into the contoso.com forest.

The Contoso.com domain has the following domain controllers:

- CRWDC01 (Windows Server 2012 R2) – Sacramento – GC and DNS*
- CRWDC02 (Windows Server 2012 R2) – Sacramento – PDC Emulator, Infrastructure Master, RID Master, Schema Master, Domain Naming Master, and DNS*
- CRWDC03 (Windows Server 2012) – Detroit – DNS
- CRWDC04 (Windows Server 2008 R2) – Miami – GC and DNS

- CRWDC05 (Windows Server 2008 R2) – Dallas – GC and DNS
- CRWDC06 (Windows Server 2008 R2) – Pittsburgh – DNS
- CRWDC07 (Windows Server 2008 R2) – Phoenix – GC and DNS
- CRWDC08 (Windows Server 2008 R2) – Seattle – DNS
- CRWDC09 (Windows Server 2008 R2) – Oklahoma City – GC and DNS
- CRWDC10 (Windows Server 2008 R2) – Portland – GC and DNS

*Virtual server running on Windows Server 2012 R2 Hyper-V

The support.contoso.com domain has the following domain controllers:

- CRWDC11 (Windows Server 2008 R2) – GC, PDC Emulator, Infrastructure Master, RID Master, and DNS

The Adatum.com forest/domain has two domain controllers:

- ARWDC01 (Windows Server 2008 R2) – GC and DNS
- ARWDC02 (Windows Server 2008 R2) – GC, PDC Emulator, Infrastructure Master, RID Master, Schema Master, Domain Naming Master, and DNS

SERVERS

For a large company with many products and designs, there are many servers throughout the various sites. As a new administrator at Contoso, file storage and access will have to be reevaluated so that the files are accessible to those users who need access while keeping the file secure. Each site (except the corporate office and call center) will have 2-4 file servers/print servers.

Within the data center are two chassis, each chassis with 4 blades running Windows Server 2012 R2 Datacenter and Hyper-V. In addition, the corporate office has the following servers:

- 4 mail servers running Microsoft Windows Server 2012 R2 and Microsoft Exchange 2013
- 4 database servers running Microsoft Windows Server 2012 R2 and Microsoft SQL 2012
- 4 content management servers running Microsoft Windows Server 2008 R2 and Microsoft SharePoint 2010 servers*
- 12 application servers running Windows Server 2008 R2, Windows Server 2012 and Windows Server 2012 R2*
- 8 internal web servers running Windows Server 2008 R2, Windows Server 2012, and Windows Server 2012 R2*
- 8 external web servers (placed in the DMZ) running Windows Server 2008 R2*
- 2 external DNS servers (placed in the DMZ) running Windows Server 2008 R2
- 2 internal DHCP servers in a failover cluster running Windows Server 2008 R2
- 5 file servers running Windows Server 2008 R2, Windows Server 2012, and Windows Server 2012 R2
- 5 file servers running Windows Server 2008 R2, Windows Server 2012, and Windows Server 2012 R2*
- 2 print servers running Windows Server 2008 R2*

*Virtual server running on Windows Server 2012 R2 Hyper-V

The call center has the following servers:

- 4 file/print servers running Windows Server 2008 R2
- 4 application servers running Windows Server 2008 R2
- 4 internal web servers running Windows Server 2008 R2
- 2 servers running Windows Server 2008 R2 and Microsoft SQL Server 2010
- 1 DHCP server running Windows Server 2008 R2

Adatum has the following virtual servers running on Hyper-V:

- 2 mail servers running Microsoft Windows Server 2008 R2 and Microsoft Exchange 2010*
- 2 database servers running Microsoft Windows Server 2008 R2 and Microsoft SQL 2008 R2*
- 2 application servers running Windows Server 2008 R2*
- 2 internal web servers running Windows Server 2008 R2*
- 2 external web servers (placed in the DMZ) running Windows Server 2008 R2*
- 1 internal DHCP server running Windows Server 2008 R2*
- 2 file servers running Windows Server 2008 R2, Windows Server 2012, and Windows Server 2012 R2*
- 2 print servers running Windows Server 2008 R2*

*Virtual server running on Windows Server 2012 R2 Hyper-V

External DNS is hosted by a web service.

NETWORK

The three buildings are connected together via 1 Gbps links. Building A has the primary Internet connection, which runs at 100 Mbps. The following sites are connected to the corporate office using 10 Mbps circuit:

- Detroit
- Miami
- Dallas
- Pittsburgh
- Phoenix
- Seattle
- Oklahoma City
- Portland
- Cleveland
- Reno
- Austin
- Albany
- Denver

The sales/consultant offices are connected to the corporate office with 3 Mbps links.

The sites are connected using Cisco routers and firewalls.

MAINTENANCE WINDOW

The call center must be able to assist customers 24/7. In addition, all external websites must be available 24/7. Maintenance and other tasks can be done only after coordinating with all stakeholders. The designated maintenance period for production systems is Saturday night. However, since some services or applications cannot be down, you may need to stage the application so that the service or application is functional. In addition, based on the needs of the various departments, sometimes systems cannot be taken down during the normal maintenance period.